Meeting Jesus

WOMEN OF FAITH FROM THE NEW TESTAMENT

by Jenna Kavonic

thegoodbook
COMPANY

Meeting Jesus

a good book guide

© Jenna Kavonic/The Good Book Company, 2006. Reprinted 2009, 2011, 2014

Series Consultants: Tim Chester, Tim Thornborough,
Anne Woodcock, Carl Laferton

The Good Book Company

Tel (UK): 0345-225-0880

Tel (int): + (44) 208-942-0880

Tel: (US): 866 244 2165

Email: admin@thegoodbook.co.uk

Websites

UK: www.thegoodbook.co.uk

N America: www.thegoodbook.com

Australia: www.thegoodbook.com.au

New Zealand: www.thegoodbook.co.nz

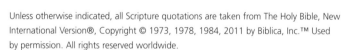

ISBN: 9781905564460

Printed in the Czech Republic

CONTENTS

Introduction: good book guides

Every Bible-study group is different—yours may take place in a church building, in a home or in a cafe, on a train, over a leisurely mid-morning coffee or squashed into a 30-minute lunch break. Your group may include new Christians, mature Christians, non-Christians, mums and tots, students, businessmen or teens. That's why we've designed these *Good Book Guides* to be flexible for use in many different situations.

Our aim in each session is to uncover the meaning of a passage, and see how it fits into the "big picture" of the Bible. But that can never be the end. We also need to appropriately apply what we have discovered to our lives. Let's take a look at what is included:

⊕ **Talkabout:** Most groups need to "break the ice" at the beginning of a session, and here's the question that will do that. It's designed to get people talking around a subject that will be covered in the course of the Bible study.

⬇ **Investigate:** The Bible text for each session is broken up into manageable chunks, with questions that aim to help you understand what the passage is about. **The Leader's Guide** contains **guidance on questions**, and sometimes ⊠ additional "follow-up" questions.

⊡ **Explore more (optional):** These questions will help you connect what you have learned to other parts of the Bible, so you can begin to fit it all together like a jig-saw; or occasionally look at a part of the passage that's not dealt with in detail in the main study.

⊡ **Apply:** As you go through a Bible study, you'll keep coming across **apply** sections. These are questions to get the group discussing what the Bible teaching means in practice for you and your church. ⊡ **Getting personal** is an opportunity for you to think, plan and pray about the changes that you personally may need to make as a result of what you have learned.

⬆ **Pray:** We want to encourage prayer that is rooted in God's word—in line with His concerns, purposes and promises. So each session ends with an opportunity to review the truths and challenges highlighted by the Bible study, and turn them into prayers of request and thanksgiving.

The **Leader's Guide** and introduction provide historical background information, explanations of the Bible texts for each session, ideas for **optional extra** activities, and guidance on how best to help people uncover the truths of God's word.

Why study Meeting Jesus?

*Blessed is she who has believed that the Lord
would fulfil his promises to her!*
Luke 1 v 45

In an age when women were considered second-class citizens, Jesus met and spent time with a surprising number of them—responding to their needs, treating them with dignity and compassion, and even seeking out those who would not normally have crossed His path. Ignoring the social restrictions of the time, He commended their faith, accepted their love and devotion, taught them and challenged them. Jesus devoted time and care to all sorts of women—the godly, the grieving, the sick, the stressed, the sinful outcasts and even those viewed as foreign "dogs".

Through these encounters, we too can discover who Jesus revealed Himself to be—the King promised by God throughout the Old Testament; the "living water"; the forgiver; the healer; the super-abundantly merciful one; the greatest teacher; the resurrection and life; and the conqueror over death. We can also learn what it means to be a woman of faith—humble, willing to obey, devoted, persevering, attentive to Jesus' words and, above all, trusting.

We will see that Jesus wasn't just being "nice" to women! He wanted to give each of them the opportunity to hear and receive His good news—that however we live, we all need God's forgiveness; that whatever we have done, we can be forgiven by God through Him.

World-wide, the good news of Jesus still transforms the lives of countless women today. By using this Good Book Guide to examine the extraordinary encounters of eight women who met Jesus, you too can learn about His liberating good news, discover what it means to have true faith, and by trusting in Him as your Lord and Saviour, experience His transforming power in your life as well.

1

Luke 1 v 26-56
FAITH THAT KNOWS GOD

⊕ talkabout

1. Think of someone that you trust. Why do you trust that person? What is it that makes them trustworthy?

⊕ investigate

Mary is an example of simple trust. She believed the unbelievable—that she, a virgin, would give birth to a son! The alternative was that God wouldn't do what He had said He would do. But she refused to believe that—that really was unbelievable! And so we read Elizabeth's words: "Blessed is she who has believed that the Lord would fulfil his promises to her!" (Luke 1 v 45). But how did Mary know that God was trustworthy? And how was she able to believe the impossible?

▶ Read Luke 1 v 26-38

2. What is unusual about the events surrounding Jesus' birth?

> **DICTIONARY**
>
> **Galilee (v 26):** a region in the north of Israel.
> **David (v 27):** King David, Israel's greatest king. God had promised one of his descendants would reign forever.
> **Jacob (v 33):** Israel.

3. Put yourself in Mary's shoes. How would you have felt in her situation?

4. Look up these Old Testament promises and explain how they are fulfilled in Jesus.

Promise	Fulfilment
2 Samuel 7 v 12-16	Luke 1 v 32-33
Genesis 12 v 1-3	Luke 1 v 54-55

5. Why do you think the angel Gabriel calls Mary "highly favoured" (v 28-33)?

6. How does Mary respond to the angel's message (v 34, 38)?

⊟ apply

7. What can we learn from Mary's wonderful example about how to respond to God in situations that are difficult to understand?

- Imagine you face a situation this week where it is hard to understand what God is doing. What would it look like for you to trust Him as Mary did? What would you do, and not do?

⊡ getting personal

It is particularly difficult to trust God when we don't understand what He is doing. We wonder why our good God will allow things that our experience tells us are likely to cause us harm or suffering. How do you react when you don't understand what God is doing? Do you trust God or do you worry? Do you pray or do you complain?

Do you face a situation like this at the moment? What do you need to do?

⊥ investigate

❯ Read Luke 1 v 39-56

8. What do you think "blessed" means (v 42, 45, 48)?

> **DICTIONARY**
>
> **Abraham (v 55):** the man from who all Israel was descended from. God had promised to bless his family, and to bless the world through his family.

9. Why did Elizabeth (v 42) and Mary (v 48-49) describe Mary as "blessed"? Is this a blessing that we can receive?

10. In verse 45 Elizabeth mentions another different kind of blessing for Mary. What is the reason for this blessing? Is this a blessing that we can receive?

11. Mary knew about God's character (v 46-50) and actions (v 51-55). That's why she could respond as she did. What does her song teach us about:

 • God's character?

 • God's actions?

12. How do you think Mary knew what God was like?

⊟ apply

13. How will knowing God and understanding His purposes, as Mary did, help us to trust and praise Him through "impossible" situations?

14. We get to know more of God's character, promises and plans by reading His word. How should this affect our attitude to reading the Bible?

⊡ getting personal

How well do you feel that you know God—His character, His actions, His promises and His plans? What can you start doing this week to get to know Him better?

⊡ explore more

> **Read Luke 8 v 19-21 and 11 v 27-28**

Who does Jesus consider to be His mother and brothers—His true family? Who, then, are truly blessed?

optional

⬆ pray

Looking back at question eleven, praise God for who He is and what He has done. Make your prayers specific and heartfelt.
Pray that God would help you to respond as Mary did, in situations where it is difficult to trust Him.

2 John 4 v 1-42
FAITH THAT RECEIVES ETERNAL LIFE

⊕ talkabout

1. What kinds of people do you tend to avoid? Why?

⊕ investigate

Long before Jesus' conversation with this Samaritan woman, shortly after the reign of the great King Solomon, the land of Israel was divided into the northern kingdom of Israel and the southern kingdom of Judah. In 722-721BC, the northern kingdom was invaded by the Assyrians, who intermarried with the Israelites and corrupted their religion, by introducing the worship of foreign gods (2 Kings 17 v 24-41).

Consequently, the Samaritans (as they were called) only held to the first five books of the Bible as Scripture. They thought that Mount Gerizim, rather than the temple in Jerusalem, was the correct place of worship. Considered unfaithful to their people (because of their history of intermarriage) and unfaithful to their religion (because of their foreign ways of worship), the Samaritans came to be utterly despised by the Jews.

❯ Read John 4 v 1-30

2. Why is the Samaritan woman surprised by Jesus' question (v 7-9, see also v 27)?

> **DICTIONARY**
>
> **Jacob (v 5):** the fore-father of all Israel. He was Abraham's grandson.

3. In verse 10 Jesus suggests that there are things this woman doesn't know—otherwise, she would have asked Jesus for "living water". What doesn't she know?

4. Look carefully at verses 10-15. Jesus and the woman are talking at cross purposes. What is the woman talking about? What is Jesus talking about?

• The woman:

• Jesus:

5. What is the gift of living water that Jesus offers her (v 14)? What is so wonderful about this gift?

• Why is water such a good image?

6. Why do you think Jesus tells her to fetch her husband?

7. Jesus and the woman are again talking at cross purposes in verses 19-24. What does the woman think is the most important thing about worship?

• What point is Jesus making?

⊡ explore more

optional

> ❯ Read John 2 v 19-22; 7 v 38-39; Ezekiel 36 v 24-27; Romans 12 v 1-2

What does it mean to worship God in spirit and truth?

Are we worshipping God when we go to church, sing and do good things? Is it possible for us not to worship God while doing these things? Why? What worship pleases God?

8. Who does Jesus reveal Himself to be in v 25-26 (see also v 42)?

9. How has this woman grown in her understanding of who Jesus is?

• v 9

• v 12

• v 19

• v 29

10. How does she respond when she begins to understand that Jesus is the Christ (v 28-30)?

11. Look through the passage and write down all the things you notice about Jesus' character. What is striking about the way He deals with this woman?

⤷ **apply**

12. What does this passage teach us about who Jesus came to save? How can you reflect this in your own life?

• How can this passage help those who feel they don't come from the right "background" to become a Christian?

⊡ **getting personal**

Think again about the kinds of people that you mentioned in question one. Are you denying people like these the opportunity to discover Jesus' offer of salvation? What can you do about that?

⬇ investigate

❯ Read John 4 v 31-42

DICTIONARY

Rabbi (v 31): teacher.

13. How do the events of v 39-42 help us to understand Jesus' words in v 34-38? What are the fields and the harvest pictures of?

➔ apply

14. Compare the end of the story (v 39-42) with the unpromising way in which this encounter began (v 7-9). Note also Jesus' words in verse 37. How can this passage encourage us to move out of our comfort zones and cross social or cultural barriers with the good news of Jesus?

⊡ getting personal

Does your will and work reflect God's (v 34)? Do you have a heart of compassion for all the lost? Are you concerned for the salvation of the world? What can you do about this?

⬆ pray

Look back at question eleven and spend some time praising God for Jesus. How have you been challenged by this passage? Talk to God about your answer.

3 Luke 7 v 36-50
FAITH THAT LOVES GREATLY

⊕ talkabout

1. Imagine someone completely forgave you for doing something terribly wrong. How would it affect your relationship with that person?

⊕ investigate

In Luke 7 v 36-50 Jesus is invited to the house of a Pharisee. The Pharisees were a group of religious leaders who taught a strict interpretation of Jewish law and had added many traditions and rules. They were well-respected and influential over ordinary people; they thought of themselves as righteous people, and were viewed as such by others. But appearances could be misleading!

> ❯ **Read Luke 7 v 36-38**

2. Look back at Luke 7 v 29-30. What do we know about Pharisees?

DICTIONARY

Reclined (v 36): lay. In Jesus' day, people lay down on couches to eat.

3. Look at v 36-38. What do we learn about the woman?

❯ Read Luke 7 v 39-50

DICTIONARY

Denarii (v 41): a coin, worth about a day's wages for a labourer.

4. What does the Pharisee think about Jesus? Why does he think this?

5. Use the table below to compare the Pharisee's actions with those of the woman.

The Pharisee	The woman
v 44	v 44
v 45	v 45
v 46	v 46

6. What do their actions show about their attitudes towards Jesus?

• The Pharisee:

• The woman:

7. Jesus tells a parable in v 40-42, which is explained in v 43-47. Who does the money-lender represent? Who do the two debtors represent? What does the parable mean?

8. Why has the woman been forgiven (v 50)?

9. What does verse 47 mean? How might it be misunderstood?

⊟ apply

10. The woman loved Jesus with a love that was considered excessive, and perhaps reckless or foolish—a lavish love pouring out a valuable perfume. Do we love Jesus the way this woman loved Him? What stops us?

▣ getting personal

Have you put your faith in Jesus for the forgiveness of all your sins? Do you feel forgiven? What do you think of Jesus now?
The woman's love for Jesus was measured by her generosity to Him and sacrifice for Him. How much are you willing to give to and sacrifice for Jesus? In what ways can you show your love for Him?

⊡ investigate

11. Look at verses 39 and 48-49. Simon and his guests are scandalised by what happens between Jesus and the woman. What do we learn about Simon and his guests from these verses?

• What do we learn about Jesus?

⊡ explore more

> ❯ **Read Luke 4 v 14-20 and 7 v 20-22**

Jesus is the one who will preach good news to the poor. From this story of the Pharisee and the sinful woman, answer the following questions:

What is the good news that Jesus brings?
Who are the poor to whom He is preaching?

⊟ apply

12. How can we be like the Pharisee in our attitude towards sinners?

• If we come across someone who is obviously a sinner, how should we treat them? And how should we not treat them?

13. Imagine you know someone who has deep and persistent guilt about past sins, which makes them doubt God's forgiveness and feel utterly unworthy of Christ's love. How can you use the things learned in this passage to help them?

⊡ getting personal

Who are you most like—the Pharisee or the woman? In what ways has this passage addressed and challenged you?

⬆ pray

Spend some time praying about what you have learned from the passage:

Thank God...
that He forgives sinful people like us.

Confess...
your sin to Him—especially attitudes that are like those of Simon, the Pharisee.

Ask...
Him to give you a greater understanding of your own sin, a better appreciation of His forgiveness, and a stronger love for Jesus.

4 Mark 5 v 24-34
FAITH THAT TRANSFORMS SUFFERING

⊕ talkabout

1. Why do you think people react to suffering in such different ways?

⊕ investigate

In Mark 1 v 32-39 Jesus tells His astonished disciples that His priority is to preach, rather than to perform miracles. This is despite the overwhelming needs of everyone in the town, who keeps coming to Him for healing. After that, every miracle that Jesus does serves a teaching purpose. The four miracles recorded in 4 v 35 – 5 v 43 are no exception. They show us the extent of Jesus' authority—over creation, evil, suffering and death. They make us ask the question: "Who is this?". This is exactly how the disciples respond (see 4 v 41).

▶ **Read Mark 5 v 24-34**

2. How bad was this woman's situation? **Read Leviticus 15 v 25-31**. How does this help us to understand the depth of her suffering (v 25-26)?

3. What is extraordinary about her healing (v 26-29)?

- What would normally be the result of this woman's physical contact with Jesus (see Leviticus 15 v 26-27)? What happens here, and what does that show us about Jesus?

4. What is remarkable about the woman's faith?

5. Look at v 30-34. Do you think that Jesus was aware of who had touched Him, and what His power had been used for (see also Luke 8 v 47)?

6. What do you notice about how Jesus treats this woman?

- Why do you think that He brings her to public attention (v 32-34)?

⤇ apply

7. Jesus not only wants us to put our faith in Him; He wants our faith in Him to be seen by others. How would you use this passage to help someone who is a secret believer in Jesus?

⊡ getting personal

If you have put your faith in Jesus, how many people around you know that? Is there anything that you should do to make your faith more public?

⊡ investigate

8. Why has the woman been healed (v 34)?
In what way could verse 34 be misunderstood?

9. Over what things does Jesus display His power?

⊡ explore more

optional

The miracle of the healing of this woman occurs in the middle of another incident, which also ends in a miracle.

▶ **Read Mark 5 v 21-23 and 35-43**

What are the similarities and differences between the two stories?

What else do we learn about Jesus' power?

In what ways do these two miracles foreshadow Jesus' death and resurrection?

⊡ apply

10. What has struck you about how this woman responds to her suffering?

• Imagine you face a difficult situation this week. Think of a particular way that you can put into practice what you have learned from this passage.

11. Some people say that if you have enough faith, you will be healed. How would you respond to that?

⊡ getting personal

What is your first response in suffering or sickness? Do you trust God to do whatever is best for you? Do you trust that He will one day deliver you from all sickness and suffering?

⊡ explore more

optional

▶ Read James 4 v 3; John 14 v 13-14, 15 v 7-8; Matthew 7 v 7-11; Romans 8 v 28-39

What reasons do these verses give us why God does not always respond to our prayers in the way in which we would like?

⊡ pray

Pray about what you have learned. Here are some ideas:

Praise God...
for His power over death, illness and suffering.

Thank God...
for Jesus' willingness to experience the power of death, so that we might have life.

Ask God...
to strengthen your faith in His power and love, particularly as you face suffering.

5 Matthew 15 v 21-28
FAITH THAT PERSEVERES

⊕ talkabout

1. Think of something in your life that you wanted to do and tried to do, but eventually gave up. Why didn't you persevere?

⊕ investigate

> **Read Matthew 15 v 21-28**

Have you ever felt that your prayers just hit the ceiling? Sometimes God does not seem to answer our needs. The Canaanite woman in this story experienced that too. She cried to Jesus for mercy but He "did not answer a word" (v 23). And yet, she wasn't discouraged; she persevered and was rewarded. Why was she able to do that? And why did Jesus treat her so strangely? Her example teaches us what we need for perseverance. We learn why God often makes us wait for an answer to our prayers, and also, why it is worth the wait!

DICTIONARY

Canaanite (v 22): the Canaanites had lived in Israel before Israel took possession of it. Throughout God's people's history, the Canaanites had been their enemies.

2. What is surprising in verse 22?

3. What do the woman's words in verse 22 show us about:

• her understanding of Jesus?

• her view of herself?

4. What has driven her to cry out to Jesus?

⤷ apply

5. What can we learn from this encounter about how God uses suffering for our good?

⤓ investigate

6. How do the disciples react to the woman's desperate request?

7. Why do you think that Jesus doesn't answer her at first (v 23a)?

8. How does she respond to this test (v 25)? What does her response show about her view of Jesus?

9. Jesus' words in v 24 and 26 sound harsh. What does He mean by them?

• verse 24 (see Matthew 10 v 5-6):

• verse 26:

10. In verse 28 Jesus praises this woman for her faith. How does her answer show faith in Jesus?

• What is remarkable about her faith?

• What have the disciples learned by seeing her faith?

→ **apply**

11. What have you learned from the Canaanite woman? How can we follow her example?

12. How do you respond when God doesn't seem to be listening to your prayer requests?

• How can this passage help you to persevere in prayer?

optional

⊡ explore more

> ❱ Read Luke 18 v 1-8

Why should we "always pray and not give up" (v 1)?

How can people misunderstand this parable? How does the example of the Canaanite woman's faith help us to understand the parable correctly?

⊡ getting personal

In what ways has your faith been tested? Has your faith risen to the challenge, as this woman's did?

Have you been encouraged to persevere in crying out to Jesus, believing that He will have mercy on you no matter who you are? What difference will that make this week?

⊡ pray

As a group:
Thank God that He always answers persevering prayer. Ask Him to help you grow in faith like that of the Canaanite woman.

On your own:
"Lord, Son of David, have mercy on me!" (v 22).
Make the Canaanite woman's prayer your own, and persevere in pleading with God, believing that He is merciful to those who have faith in Jesus.

6 Luke 10 v 38-42
FAITH THAT LISTENS TO JESUS

⊕ talkabout

1. What things do you make time to do each day, no matter how busy you are? Why do you make those things a priority?

⊕ investigate

❯ Read Luke 10 v 38-42

Every Christian feels it—we want to spend time with God by reading His word, but we keep getting distracted by so many other urgent things. The tension that we see between Martha and Mary is the same tension that we can feel within ourselves—the struggle for priority between doing and listening.

2. What can we learn from Martha from verse 38?

3. What can we learn about Mary from verse 39?
See also John 11 v 1-2, 32 and 12 v 1-7.

4. What did Martha get wrong?

• What do you think were the "many things" (v 41) that Martha was worried about?

• What was the "one" thing (v 42) that she needed to be concerned about?

⤷ apply

5. How can we listen to Jesus now?

• Why is it so important to make spending time in God's word our greatest concern?

6. How do we get distracted from listening to Jesus? What kind of things do we worry about?

- What can we do to make sure that our time of reading and reflecting on God's word doesn't get squeezed out by other things?

⊡ **getting personal**

Do you love and enjoy spending time with the Lord, as Mary did? When you find yourself worried and upset, do you turn to God and what He says? How can you cultivate a fresh delight in His word?

⊡ **explore more**

optional

▶ **Read Acts 6 v 1-6**

What was the highest priority for the apostles in the first days of the church? Why do you think this was so important?

How should this priority be reflected in our churches today?

⊡ **investigate**

7. Compare the two women. What do you find most striking?

8. Why does Jesus commend Mary's listening rather than Martha's service?

9. How does Jesus deal with the two women?

⤷ apply

10. Why do you think women like Mary are so rare?

- What is it about Mary that safeguards her from charges of laziness or slackness in hospitality?

11. It is good to serve Christ; but how can we know whether our serving has become more important to us than listening to Him?

⊡ getting personal

Your personality may be that of a "doer", rather like Martha (who was also commendably hard-working, dedicated, efficient, practical and hospitable). Or you may be more of a "listener", like Mary.

What sins and failings may present more of a danger to you than to others, because of your personality type? What can you do about that? How has this passage challenged or encouraged you in this area?

⊡ pray

Thank God...
for the privilege of knowing Jesus.

Confess...
if you have failed to spend enough time with Him.

Ask...
the Lord to give you Mary's strengths—to make you more loving, more devoted and more attentive. Ask Him to protect you from Martha's failings—to make you less distracted, less busy and less worried about many unnecessary things.

7 John 11 v 1-44
FAITH THAT OVERCOMES DEATH

⊕ talkabout

1. All of us at some stage have experienced (or will) the death of a loved one. How do different people deal with the shock and pain involved?
How can we prepare ourselves for this experience?

⊕ investigate

> **Read John 11 v 1-16**

In the scientifically knowledgeable, technologically advanced 21st century, death remains the greatest enemy of the human race. Death is socially unacceptable, medically uncontrollable, personally incomprehensible, seemingly capricious in the way that it selects its victims, inevitable, irreversible, terrifying, utterly destructive and absolutely final. It is the one certainty that we all face, regardless of how we have lived and whether we have ignored and disobeyed, or loved and devoted ourselves to God.

"Where is God when death strikes? Is He really in control? Does He really love me?" These questions plague many of our minds when tragedy comes our way. Here is the answer!

2. How did Jesus feel about Lazarus and his sisters (verses 3 and 5, see also verse 36)?

3. Why did Jesus delay going to Bethany to see Lazarus (v 6)?
- verse 4:

- verses 11-15:

❯ Read John 11 v 17-37

4. How did Martha and Mary handle their brother's death (v 20-22, 32)?

5. What was Martha's hope (v 22-24)? Compare verse 39.

- In eternity, what will Lazarus, Martha and Mary be more thankful for—the resurrection at Bethany, or the resurrection at the last day?

6. What did Jesus explain to Martha in verses 25-26?

7. In v 26 Jesus asked Martha: "Do you believe this?" How did Martha respond? What does this show us about true belief?

⠢ explore more

▶ Read John 5 v 24, Ephesians 2 v 1-5 and Colossians 2 v 13-14

What does it mean to be "dead" according to these verses?

What does it mean to be "alive"?

In the following verses, what do we discover about the way the physical death of a Christian is different from that of a non-Christian?

- *1 Corinthians 15 v 20 (compare Matthew 9 v 18-19 and 23-26)*

- *1 Corinthians 15 v 55-57*

- *Philippians 1 v 21-23*

Why is the experience of death transformed for a Christian (see Hebrews 2 v 9)?

Now explain Jesus' words in v 25-26.
"Whoever believes in me will live, even though they die" (v 25b).
"Whoever lives by believing in me will never die" (v 26).

8. Jesus knew that "this illness [would] not end in death" (v 4, see also v 11-13). Why, then, did Jesus weep, do you think (v 33-35)?

9. What did the Jews conclude about Jesus?

- verse 36:

- verse 37:

⊟ apply

10. What can we learn from Martha and Mary about how to respond to death and bereavement?

11. What can we learn from the Jews about how *not* to respond to tragedy?

12. How are Jesus' words to Martha in verses 23-26 both a comfort and a warning to those who have suffered loss?

⊡ getting personal

Have you suffered personal loss? If so, how has this passage been a comfort and a help to you?

Does the heartbreak of others bring tears to your eyes, as it did to Jesus? What can you do to bring them hope?

⊡ investigate

> ❯ **Read John 11 v 38-44**

13. What did Jesus mean when He said that Martha would "see the glory of God" (v 40)? How is God glorified through this miracle?

⊡ apply

14. Where can we see God's glory most fully displayed?
See also 12 v 23-24, 31-33.

• What difference should that make to our lives this week?

⊡ getting personal

Have you seen the glory of God in Jesus' own death and resurrection?

Do you believe that He has power over your death, and power to give you life—eternal life?

How does that make you live differently from the people around you?

⊡ pray

Spend some time praising God together. Praise Him for Jesus' death and resurrection; for His power over death and His power to give life; for the difference that He has made to your own death.

Thank God for His sovereignty and love. Even though you may not see His power or feel His love when you are hurting, you can trust that He is in control and that He is good. Ask Him to help you to cling to Him, as Martha and Mary did.

8 John 20 v 1-18
FAITH THAT SHARES THE GOOD NEWS

⊕ talkabout

1. When something extraordinary happens to you, do you tend to talk about it or keep it to yourself?

⊕ investigate

> **Read John 20 v 1-18**

2. Looking at verses 1-9, what evidence is there in this passage that Jesus was physically raised from the dead?

DICTIONARY

Other disciple, the one Jesus loved (v 2): John, who wrote this Gospel.

   • v 1 (compare Mark 16 v 1-4; Matthew 28 v 2):

   • v 2:

   • v 3-7:

3. Compare the ways in which "the other disciple" and Mary reacted to the empty tomb.

   • The other disciple:

   • Mary:

⮕ apply

4. At first, Mary failed to believe in the resurrection despite the evidence she had seen. Why is it still important to have evidence for the resurrection?

• Why isn't the evidence sufficient for people to believe, do you think?

5. People who don't believe in the resurrection need other theories to explain the disappearance of Jesus' body from the tomb. What explanations are commonly given? How can you use the evidence in this passage to contradict these theories?

⊡ explore more

> **▶ Read 1 Corinthians 15 v 12-28**

What is the significance of the resurrection? Or, to put it another way, what would it mean if Jesus had never been raised from the dead? Base your answers on:
• *v 14-16*
• *v 17-19*
• *v 22-26*

What convinces you personally that Jesus really was raised from the dead? (If you're not convinced, what are your reasons for believing that He wasn't raised?)

If you struggle with belief, have you ever prayed for the Holy Spirit to open your eyes to the truth? If you do believe, have you ever thanked God for His gift of faith to you?

⊡ **investigate**

6. **Read Luke 8 v 2-3.** What can we learn about Mary Magdalene here?

7. How is Mary's deep love for Jesus seen in this story (v 10-18)?

8. At what point does Mary believe that Jesus is alive (v 14-16)?
Read verses 24-28. How does Thomas' experience compare with Mary's?

9. Jesus' words "Do not hold on to me" (v 17a) seem a bit heartless. Why do you think Jesus says this to Mary?

10. What does He command her to do instead?

11. Look at verse 19 and **Luke 24 v 11**. What things must have made it hard for Mary to do as Jesus said?

⮕ apply

12. In what way does this story show how we should relate to the risen Lord in this world?

13. Why do we so often fail to tell others about Jesus' death and resurrection?

• How can we bring the subject of the resurrection into our everyday conversations with non-Christians?

⊡ getting personal

Do you think you have grasped and experienced how astonishing and life-changing these events are?

How can you begin to follow Mary's example this week? When and where can you try to speak about Jesus' resurrection?

↑ pray

Think about what has struck you most from this session and turn that into prayer.

Praise God...
for the resurrection and for all that it means to you. Praise Him that death is defeated, your sin can be forgiven and you can have eternal life beyond the grave!

Ask God...
to give you the courage to proclaim the good news to someone that you know. And pray for that person to believe the gospel.

Meeting Jesus

Women of faith from the New Testament

LEADER'S GUIDE

Leader's Guide

INTRODUCTION

Leading a Bible study can be a bit like herding cats—everyone has a different idea of what the passage could be about, and a different line of enquiry that they want to pursue. But a good group leader is more than someone who just referees this kind of discussion. You will want to:

- correctly understand and handle the Bible passage. But also…

- encourage and train the people in your group to do this for themselves. Don't fall into the trap of spoon-feeding people by simply passing on the information in the Leader's Guide. Then…

- make sure that no Bible study is finished without everyone knowing how the passage is relevant for them. What changes do you all need to make in the light of the things you have been learning? And finally…

- encourage the group to turn all that has been learned and discussed into prayer.

Your Bible-study group is unique, and you are likely to know better than anyone the capabilities, backgrounds and circumstances of the people you are leading. That's why we've designed these guides with a number of optional features. If they're a quiet bunch, you might want to spend longer on talkabout. If your time is limited, you can choose to skip explore more, or get people to look at these questions at home. Can't get enough of Bible study? Well, some studies have optional extra homework projects. As leader, you can adapt and select the material to the needs of your particular group.

So what's in the Leader's Guide? The main thing that this Leader's Guide will help you to do is to understand the major teaching points in the passage you are studying, and how to apply them. As well as guidance on the questions, the Leader's Guide for each session contains the following important sections:

THE BIG IDEA

One key sentence will give you the main point of the session. This is what you should be aiming to have fixed in people's minds as they leave the Bible study. And it's the point you need to head back towards when the discussion goes off at a tangent.

SUMMARY

An overview of the passage, including plenty of useful historical background information.

OPTIONAL EXTRA

Usually this is an introductory activity that ties in with the main theme of the Bible study, and is designed to "break the ice" at the beginning of a session. Or it may be a "homework project" that people can tackle during the week.

So let's take a look at the various different features of a Good Book Guide:

⊕ talkabout

Each session kicks off with a discussion question, based on the group's opinions or experiences. It's designed to get people talking and thinking in a general way about the main subject of the Bible study.

⊌ investigate

The first thing you and your group need to know is what the Bible passage is about, which is the purpose of these questions. But watch out—people may come up with answers based on their experiences or teaching they have heard in the past, without referring to the passage at all. It's amazing how often we can get through a Bible study without actually looking at the Bible! If you're stuck for an answer, the Leader's Guide contains guidance on questions. These are the answers to direct your group to. This information isn't meant to be read out to people—ideally, you want them to discover these answers from the Bible for themselves. Sometimes there are optional follow-up questions (see ⊗ in guidance on questions) to help you help your group get to the answer.

⊡ explore more

These questions generally point people to other relevant parts of the Bible. They are useful for helping your group to see how the passage fits into the "big picture" of the whole Bible. These sections are OPTIONAL—only use them if you have time. Remember that it's better to finish in good time having really grasped one big thing from the passage, than to try and cram everything in.

⊟ apply

We want to encourage you to spend more time working at application—too often, it is simply tacked on at the end. In the Good Book Guides, apply sections are mixed in with the investigate sections of the study. We hope that people will realise that application is not just an optional extra, but rather, the whole purpose of studying the

Bible. We do Bible study so that our lives can be changed by what we hear from God's word. If you skip the application, the Bible study hasn't achieved its purpose.

These questions draw out practical lessons that we can all learn from the Bible passage. You can review what has been learned so far, and think about practical differences that this should make in our churches and our lives. The group gets the opportunity to talk about what they personally have learned.

⊡ getting personal

These can be done at home, but it is well worth allowing a few moments of quiet reflection during the study for each person to think and pray about specific changes they need to make in their own lives. Why not have a time for reporting back at the beginning of the following session, so that everyone can be encouraged and challenged by one another to make application a priority?

⬆ pray

In Acts 4 v 25-30 the first Christians quoted Psalm 2 as they prayed in response to the persecution of the apostles by the Jewish religious leaders. Today however, it's not as common for Christians to base prayers on the truths of God's word as it once was. As a result, our prayers tend to be weak, superficial and self-centred rather than bold, visionary and God-centred.

The prayer section is based on what has been learned from the Bible passage. How different our prayer times would be if we were genuinely responding to what God has said to us through His word.

1 Luke 1 v 25-56
FAITH THAT KNOWS GOD

THE BIG IDEA
If we know God—His character, His actions, His promises and His plans—we will be able to trust and praise Him through situations that we don't understand.

SUMMARY
Mary lived at a time when Israel had not yet seen the fulfilment of various OT prophecies that promised a special king (eg: 2 Samuel 7 v 12-16). After receiving a message from God through the angel Gabriel, Mary believed that she would give birth to that king, fulfilling the prophecy of Isaiah 7 v 14, that a virgin would give birth to a son named Immanuel, even though she did not understand how that would happen. And despite the shame that it would bring, she was able to rejoice because she knew God—what He was like, how He had acted in the past and what He had promised for the future.

Mary's faith was simple: she simply believed God's words. That is faith. And that is why she is the first character in *Meeting Jesus*.

GUIDANCE ON QUESTIONS
1. Think of someone that you trust. Why do you trust that person? What is it that makes them trustworthy? Faith is not blind. Faith and knowledge go hand in hand. We won't trust a person unless we know something about them. We tell our children not to trust strangers. To really trust someone, they will need to have proved they keep their word. This question prepares people for one of the key points of this session, which is that we cannot trust God if we do not know Him.

2. What is unusual about the events surrounding Jesus' birth? The unusual events that preceded Jesus' birth suggested that He was going to be an unusual man:
- The messenger was unusual—an angel announced His birth (v 26-28)! Although this was not the first time that the birth of a child was announced by an angel, only significant biblical characters were introduced into the world in this way.
- The message was unusual—essentially, that the child to be born would be the undying King of an unending kingdom (v 29-33).
- Mary's conception was unusual—a virgin conceived by the power of the Holy Spirit—and as a result, her child was called the Son of God (v 34-35).
- The circumstances were unusual—Mary's relative Elizabeth had also conceived miraculously (v 36-37).
- Jesus' birth was planned and predicted!

3. Put yourself in Mary's shoes. How would you have felt in her situation? A young girl, not yet married, falls pregnant… It was a scandal! It is hard to imagine the disgrace and humiliation that Mary would have had to endure.

4. Look up these Old Testament promises and explain how they are fulfilled in Jesus.
- Promise (2 Sam 7 v 12-16): One of David's descendants will rule for ever.
- Fulfilment (Luke 1 v 32-33): Jesus is descended from David and "his kingdom will never end".
- Promise (Genesis 12 v 1-3): God will bless

Abraham's descendants and all people through them.

• Fulfilment (Luke 1 v 54-55): Mary knows that her child is the one through whom those promises will come true.

5. Why do you think the angel Gabriel calls Mary "highly favoured" (v 28-31)?

In v 28 the angel called Mary "highly favoured". Because Mary didn't understand why she was greeted in this way, it troubled her (v 29). But in v 30-33, the angel explained: "You will conceive and give birth to a son…" Mary was favoured because she would give birth to Jesus. She was favoured because of who her son would be (the promised King) and what her son would do (reign forever), not because of who she was or what she had done.

⊻

• **What would most people think was the reason why God favoured Mary in this way?** Most people would probably believe that Mary was favoured by God because she was godly or because she loved Him—they would expect that something good in Mary caused God to respond positively to her.

• **What can we discover about the reason why God favoured Mary in this way?** The passage doesn't give a reason. But from Mary's troubled response in v 29, it seems that Mary herself knew that there was nothing about her that would cause God to respond in this way—she certainly didn't expect any special favour from God. See also v 38. Rather, God had chosen to act in grace, by giving her this vital role in His great plan of salvation, of which she was undeserving.

• **What wrong impression do people have of Mary, and of God, because**

they fail to understand correctly the reason why Mary was said to be favoured by God? Many people believe that Mary must have been especially saintly to be chosen by God in this way, but the Bible never treats her as anything other than an ordinary woman. This also suggests a false view of God ie: He favours only good people. This is very far from the teaching of the Bible: God chooses to show favour to people, not according to what they are like—they are, anyway, always undeserving—but according to His gracious character and His sovereign purposes eg: Romans 3 v 23-24; 1 John 4 v 10.

6. How does Mary respond to the angel's message (v 34, 38)?

She asks *how* it will happen, but she doesn't disbelieve *that* it will happen (v 34). By verse 38, she is willing to put herself and her future entirely in God's hands.

⊻

• **Both Mary and Zechariah questioned the angel (v 18, 34), but in what way were their attitudes different?** Mary and Zechariah both had been told that they would have a son. And in both cases this was humanly impossible—Zechariah's wife, Elizabeth, was old and barren (v 7) and Mary was a virgin (v 27)! Naturally, both ask the question "How…?" But there is a fundamental difference between the two. Behind Zechariah's question was unbelief, whereas behind Mary's question was lack of understanding. But despite the fact that she did not understand how she would conceive, she believed (v 45) and accepted (v 38) that she would. And, despite the shame it would bring upon her, she willingly surrendered herself to

God's will without complaining. On the contrary, she praised God (v 46-55)!

7. APPLY: What can we learn from Mary's wonderful example about how to respond to God in situations that are difficult to understand?

- **How does Mary's example help us to understand what it means to "trust in the LORD with all your heart and lean not on your own understanding" (Proverbs 3 v 5)?**
- **Mary responded to the angel's message by saying: "I am the Lord's servant" (v 38). How was Mary's response servant-like? What do God's servants look like?**

Mary is an example for us to follow. She lived by the words of Proverbs 3 v 5: "Trust in the LORD with all your heart and lean not on your own understanding". Even when we don't understand what God is doing, we should respond by trusting God. Trusting God does not mean that we cannot question Him—Mary did. But it does mean believing His promises, even when His word appears to be inconsistent with our experience—Mary believed God even though no virgin had ever experienced childbirth before. And it means accepting God's will without complaint—Mary submitted to the Lord as His servant (v 38), without further worry or resentment.

8. What do you think "blessed" means (v 42, 45, 48)? To be blessed means to receive an undeserved gift from God.

9. Why did Elizabeth (v 42) and Mary (v 48-49) describe Mary as "blessed"?

Is this a blessing that we can receive? Verse 49 tells us why "blessed" is an accurate description of Mary, rather than explaining why God has blessed her. Mary is blessed because God has done great things for her (v 49), by choosing her to be the mother of this special child who would be called the Son of God.

As we have already seen in Q5, Mary was not blessed because of anything that she had done. Blessing, by definition, is undeserved. Mary herself was deeply aware of this. She refers to her "humble state" (v 48)—she was humble, lowly, unworthy. The birth of Jesus was a unique event and, in this sense, no one else will be "blessed" in the way that Mary was.

- **How does Mary speak about herself (v 48)?**

10. In verse 45 Elizabeth mentions another different kind of blessing for Mary. What is the reason for this blessing? Is this a blessing that we can receive? Elizabeth speaks of the blessing that Mary receives because of her faith—her belief that what the Lord had said to her would be accomplished (v 45).

This is not the blessing of giving birth to the Son of God—God had already chosen Mary for this task, before she knew anything about His plan, let alone believed that it would happen. Elizabeth is speaking of a subsequent blessing that results from Mary's absolute trust in the Lord, despite the apparent impossibility of the promise and the threat of scandal that could fall on her. All believers can share in this kind of blessing when they show the same trust in God as Mary. In Luke 11 v 27-28 Jesus indicates that this kind of blessing is much more important (see Explore More).

Note that faith is simply trusting in what God has done; it is nothing that we do ourselves. In fact, trust implies that we give up reliance on our own actions or merits.

11. Mary knew about God's character (v 46-50) and actions (v 51-55). That's why she could respond as she did. What does her song teach us about:

• **God's character?** He is compassionate (v 48), holy (v 49), merciful (v 50), and powerful (v 51).

• **God's actions?** The "mighty deeds" to which Mary was referring (v 51) were God's powerful acts of salvation in the Old Testament eg: the exodus. His holiness is seen in His treatment of the "proud" and the "rich"— those who don't acknowledge their spiritual poverty (v 51-53); He judges them justly. And mercy is seen in His treatment of the "humble" and the "hungry" (v 52-53); He shows kindness toward them.

12. How do you think Mary knew what God was like? Mary used Old Testament language in v 50–55. She had evidently read and memorised the Scriptures. She had become familiar with what had been recorded of God's dealings with His people and so had come to know God. It was because she knew God, through what He had revealed about Himself in His word, that she could trust Him.

13. APPLY: How will knowing God and understanding His purposes, as Mary did, help us to trust and praise Him through "impossible" situations? First, we cannot trust God unless we know what He is like. Unless we know that God is sovereign and good, powerful and holy, just and merciful, we cannot trust Him.

Second, we cannot rejoice in an otherwise difficult situation unless we understand something of His plans, purposes and promises. There was much that Mary did not understand (v 34), but she did understand that God was fulfilling His promises to bless His people (v 54-55). Because of this, she was able to look beyond her situation and praise God.

14. APPLY: We get to know more of God's character, promises and plans by reading His word. How should this affect our attitude to reading the Bible? God has chosen to reveal Himself to us through His word. We cannot know God, or His plans and purposes, unless we spend time reading and reflecting upon His word, as Mary did. That is why it is so important and valuable to read it every day! When we read the Bible, our attitude should not be to discharge a duty or to fill our minds with knowledge. We should read it wanting to know and understand God more, and expecting to be taught how to handle the situations in which we find ourselves!

EXPLORE MORE

In Luke 8 v 19-21 and 11 v 27-28, who does Jesus consider to be His mother and brothers—His true family? Who, then, are truly blessed? In Luke 8 v 19-21 Jesus redefined His family. He considered those who "hear God's word and put it into practice" as His true family, rather than His biological mother and brothers. In Luke 11 v 27-28 Jesus responded to a woman (who had called Mary blessed simply because she was His biological mother) by saying: "Blessed rather are those who hear the word of God and obey it". We should not think of Mary more highly than Jesus did. Yes, to give birth to Jesus was a blessing, but according to Him, to hear and obey God is a far greater blessing. This is the blessing that we can all share with Mary (see Q10).

OPTIONAL EXTRA

There is a lot of false teaching about Mary. For example, Catholics teach that Mary was sinless and that she was blessed because of her own merits. But to be blessed means to receive an undeserved gift. And Mary herself gave all the glory to God. It is true that she was blessed. The angel Gabriel addressed her as "highly favoured". Her relative Elizabeth said to her, "Blessed are you among women". And she herself sang, "All generations will call me blessed". But she was blessed simply because she had been chosen, undeservedly, to bear Jesus, and then she was blessed because she trusted the Lord in that difficult situation. It may be helpful to spend some time discussing this if there are people in your group who have been exposed to this false teaching.

---

2 John 4 v 1–42
FAITH THAT RECEIVES ETERNAL LIFE

THE BIG IDEA

Jesus offers eternal life to a religious, moral and social outcast, and she responds by spreading the news about Him.

SUMMARY

Jesus offers a sinful Samaritan woman eternal life and challenges her to become a true worshipper. This is a surprise to His disciples and to the woman herself, because she is a moral, religious and social outcast. This ministry to outcasts is God's will and work.

Note: This is a long and full passage, and has a lot to teach us about true worship, and about evangelism. Try to limit discussion about worship to Q7 and the Explore More section (if you have time to look at it), and discussion about Jesus' method of evangelism to Q11, so that the main message will be clear and convicting.

GUIDANCE ON QUESTIONS

1. What kind of people do you tend to avoid? Why? The purpose of this question is to expose the thinking that lies behind the reasons why we avoid talking to certain people, either at all or about Jesus—thinking that will be challenged by the passage.

- **Are there any groups of people we personally find offensive?** You could mention some groups that many would be reluctant to mix with eg: alcoholics, drug addicts, immigrants, those of other faiths like Muslims, disabled and learning disabled people, the very old or very young etc.

Or, it may be that people in your group are happy to mix with anyone, but find it difficult to share the gospel with certain types, in which case use the supplementary question below.

⌄

• What kind of people do you avoid sharing the gospel with? Why?

2. Why is the Samaritan woman surprised by Jesus' question (v 7-9, see also v 27)? By speaking to this woman, Jesus was doing what was considered socially unacceptable. First, a Jew would not talk to a Samaritan because of the disagreements and hostility that existed between them. (The Samaritans originated from the northern kingdom of Israel, one of two kingdoms into which the original land of Israel divided after the reign of King Solomon. In 722-721 BC, the northern kingdom was invaded by the Assyrians, who intermarried with the Israelites and corrupted their religion, by introducing the worship of foreign gods (2 Kings 17 v 24-41). The Jews, who thought of themselves as "pure" in both race and religion, considered the Samaritans, by contrast, to be corrupt.) Second, it was seen as unacceptable for a male Jew to speak with a woman in public.

3. In verse 10 Jesus suggests that there are things this woman doesn't know—otherwise, she would have asked Jesus for "living water". What doesn't she know? The woman doesn't know who Jesus is or what He can give her (Notice in v 10 that the gift of God—"living water"—is given by Jesus; He is claiming to be God!). If she had known who Jesus was, she would have asked Him for what He alone could give her—eternal life. Throughout His conversation with the Samaritan woman, Jesus' concern is to reveal Himself and His gift to her.

4. Look carefully at verses 10-15. Jesus and the woman are talking at cross purposes. What is the woman talking about? What is Jesus talking about?
• **The woman:** physical water.
• **Jesus:** water as an image of eternal life. The Samaritan woman misunderstands Jesus because she is thinking in physical rather than spiritual terms. Our thinking tends to be dictated by the needs, concerns and demands of this world. This often causes us to misunderstand Jesus because His thoughts, free from those constraints, differ from ours.

5. What is the gift of living water that Jesus offers her (v 14)? What is so wonderful about this gift? Unlike ordinary water, which cannot sustain life permanently, Jesus' gift of "living water" leads to eternal life.
Living water supplies our need and satisfies us forever—"whoever drinks the water I give them will never thirst" (v 14).
It transforms us from within and gives us eternal life—"the water I give them will become in them a spring of water welling up to eternal life" (v 14).
By contrast, life in this world is often dissatisfying and unfulfilling, and even when we find contentment, it doesn't last. But Jesus can give us the life we all long for—true happiness can be found in Him.

• **Why is water such a good image?** It is one of the most basic of human needs, without which we would die in a few days (the daily grind of collecting water would ensure that the woman clearly understood the desirability of this once-for-all "living water"); water produces astonishing transformation, growth and fruitfulness (think of what happens after rainfall in a desert); water is cleansing; water is pleasing and refreshing to the senses (think of oases or the importance of water features in gardens).

- **What is eternal life?** This is not just life that goes on for ever, but rather, life as God first created it—living in a relationship with God of dependence, trust and love, and receiving from Him every blessing imaginable.
- **APPLY: Do you really believe that true contentment can only be found in Jesus? Is this reflected in your thinking and in your pursuits? Where are you searching for satisfaction and fulfilment?**

6. Why do you think Jesus tells her to fetch her husband? While revealing Himself through His supernatural knowledge of her (see v 18-19, 29), Jesus also confronts the woman with her sin. But notice how He gives her the opportunity to "own up" to Him, rather than tackling the issue head-on. Naturally, she tries to avoid this sensitive issue—and the guilt and hurt she feels about it—by changing the subject. She knows that she is a woman of questionable moral character, having had five husbands and now in an illegitimate relationship. The fact that Jesus is fully aware of her sinfulness makes His offer of eternal life to her all the more astonishing.

- Why do you think the Samaritan woman changes the subject in v 20?

7. Jesus and the woman are again talking at cross purposes in verses 19-24. What does the woman think is the

most important thing about worship? The Samaritans maintained that God could be worshipped on Mount Gerizim—"this mountain" (v 21)—whereas the Jews insisted that He should be worshipped only at the temple in Jerusalem. The woman is aware that Jesus is a Jew (v 9), but also believes that He is a prophet, and so she takes the opportunity to find out His view on this controversy. For her, the most important issue is the question of who is right about where to worship God.

- **What point is Jesus making?** Although the woman brings up a controversial subject, Jesus doesn't focus on what divides Jews and Samaritans (although He confirms that the Jews are right and that the Samaritans were ignorant about where to worship). Instead, He points out what would unite them—true worship. Jesus shows us that the most important issue is that people must worship God in spirit and truth (see Explore More below).

EXPLORE MORE
What does it mean to worship God in spirit and truth?
John 2 v 19-22: Jesus referred to His body as the temple, suggesting that true worship would no longer be located in a place but in a person. We can only worship God in and through Jesus.
John 7 v 38-39: By the phrase "living water" Jesus meant the Spirit. To worship "in spirit and in truth" means more than "sincerely"; it means that we can only worship God with the help of the Holy Spirit.
Ezekiel 36 v 24-27: God had promised a time when He would cleanse, renew and enable His people to live for Him, by putting His Spirit in them. In John 4 v 23 Jesus announced that such a time had come.
Romans 12 v 1-2: To worship God is to live

holy lives that please God, no matter what the cost. It involves offering our bodies to carry out His will.

Are we worshipping God when we go to church, sing and do good things? Is it possible for us not to worship God while doing these things? Why? What worship pleases God? Worship, although it includes going to church, singing and good deeds, is much more than these things—it is about living for God. If we do not live for God and strive to be holy, then we are not worshipping God, despite the good or religious things we do.

8. Who does Jesus reveal Himself to be in v 25-26 (see also v 42)? The Samaritans, who regarded only the first five books of the Bible as Scripture, were awaiting a prophet who would "explain everything" to them (Deuteronomy 18 v 17-19). Jesus said: "I, the one speaking to you—I am he" (v 26). He revealed Himself to be the Messiah (the promised Saviour-King and the Saviour of the world (v 42)—including Samaritans, women and sinners.

9. How has this woman grown in her understanding of who Jesus is?
- **v 9:** The Samaritan woman refers to Jesus as no more than "a Jew".
- **v 12:** Her question "Are you greater than our father Jacob?" implies that the answer in her mind is "No".
- **v 19:** She acknowledges that He is a prophet.
- **v 29:** She dares to wonder whether He is the Messiah.

10. How does she respond when she begins to understand that Jesus is the Christ (v 28-30)? When the woman understands who Jesus is and what He can give her, she abandons her water jar

(perhaps indicating that she has realised her spiritual need over and above her physical need) to spread the news about Jesus in the town.

- **APPLY: Do you know Jesus and what He can give you?**
- **What do you consider your greatest need? Is this reflected in your life?**
- **How can we be like this woman in our response to Jesus?**

11. Look through the passage and write down all the things you notice about Jesus' character. What is striking about the way He deals with this woman? There are many things that could be said at this point: Jesus puts compassion for this woman before social convention; He is interested in this one individual; He initiates the conversation with her; He is single-minded in His concern to reveal Himself to her and offer her eternal life; He understands her dissatisfaction and guilt; He speaks in terms that are relevant to her; He is gentle and yet uncompromising in exposing her ignorance and sin; etc.

- **What practical lessons for evangelism can we learn from Jesus' interaction with this woman?** For example:
  - Just as Jesus initiated conversation with the woman, we should be the ones who break through social, religious and cultural barriers, and start talking about Jesus with people, rather than waiting for them to approach us with questions.
  - Just as Jesus refused to be distracted by the controversial question about worship, we should focus on clearly explaining who Jesus is and why He came.

Discussion about evolution, for example, is not evangelism.

- Just as Jesus used the image of living water to attract the woman to the gospel, we need to present the gospel in a way that is relevant to the situations of the people we are speaking to.
- We can learn from Jesus that we should neither avoid mention of people's sin, nor constantly highlight it, but rather, deal sensitively and compassionately with these issues.

12. APPLY: What does this passage teach us about who Jesus came to save? How can you reflect this in your own life? The aim of this question is to challenge people to examine whether or not they really believe that Jesus came to save everyone, and if that belief has impacted their evangelism. It can also expose the prejudices that we all have against those we might disapprove of. For example, do we really believe that Jesus came to save Muslims, or do we believe that Muslims will be saved through their Islamic religion? Would we be willing to associate with a prostitute, share the gospel with a drug dealer or invite a beggar to church? **Note:** Some people may say that they are not gifted at talking to certain types of people eg: alcoholics or foreigners. This view seems to conflate being a witness and using your gift in the church. While only some people in the New Testament church were specially gifted in evangelism (see Ephesians 4 v 11), all Christians were witnesses and spoke about Jesus as they had opportunity (see Acts 8 v 1, 4; 1 Peter 3 v 15).

- **How can this passage help those who feel they don't come from the right "background" to become a Christian?** Some people automatically exclude themselves from invitations to find out

about the Christian faith because they think that their background automatically rules out any possibility of becoming a Christian. For example, many Asians view Christianity as a western religion, and imagine that becoming a Christian must be tantamount to giving up or even turning against their own culture. Family tradition or way of life can pose similar obstacles in people's thinking. Some may feel that they are not worthy of the eternal life that Jesus offers; others cannot envisage being able to live like a Christian. This encounter between Jesus and the Samaritan woman should give us confidence that all these views of Christianity are unfounded. You may like to give your group time to discuss how to approach such people.

- **Do we really believe that Jesus came to offer salvation to everyone, and that anyone can be saved? What about Muslims? Religious terrorists? Prostitutes? Drug dealers? Beggars?**
- **Why, then, don't we share the gospel with everyone, including these kinds of people?**

13. How do the events of v 39-42 help us to understand Jesus' words in v 34-38? What are the fields and the harvest pictures of? "I tell you, open your eyes and look at the fields! They are ripe for harvest" (v 35). Had the disciples opened their eyes, they would have seen a town in Samaria—a town in which many Samaritans were ready to believe! "Even now the one who reaps draws a wage and harvests a crop for eternal life…" (v 36). As Jesus said these words, the Samaritans heard and believed the woman's testimony about Him (v 28-30, 39). Clearly, the fields and the harvest were pictures of the Samaritans and the work that Jesus was doing with them. The "others", or the sowers, that Jesus referred to in v 37-38 were the prophets, the last of whom was John the Baptist. Jesus and His disciples "reaped the benefits of their labour" (v 38).

14. APPLY: Compare the end of the story (v 39-42) with the unpromising way in which this encounter began (v 7-9). Note also Jesus' words in verse 37. How can this passage encourage us to move out of our comfort zones and cross social or cultural barriers with the good news of Jesus? From Jesus' conversation with just one—initially wary—woman, many Samaritans come to believe in Jesus. We should be encouraged by this to take every opportunity to share the gospel of Jesus, no matter how unpromising the situation appears to be, because who knows what

the results of our faithfulness will be? Jesus' statement that "One sows and another reaps" (v 37) suggests that it is always worth sharing the gospel, even when we do not see people turning to Jesus, because without the work of "sowing", there can be no "reaping" later on. By telling us that "the sower and the reaper may be glad together" (v 36), Jesus is indicating that the sower's contribution to the harvest is as important as the reaper's.

OPTIONAL EXTRA
Make a list of people who you might have an opportunity to share the gospel with. Think about how you can initiate a conversation and what you might say in the light of Jesus' example. Prayerfully consider their needs and concerns, and how you can make the gospel relevant and appealing to them. But don't stop there—be alert and bold enough to use every opportunity!

---

3 Luke 7 v 36-50
FAITH THAT LOVES GREATLY

THE BIG IDEA
The deeper our awareness of our sin and appreciation of Jesus' forgiveness, the greater our love for Him will be.

SUMMARY
Jesus compared and exposed the attitudes of a self-righteous Pharisee and a sinful woman. The sinful woman poured an expensive bottle of perfume on Jesus' feet. This was an expression of gratitude and love for which she was commended. By contrast, the Pharisee was rebuked because he condemned Jesus for tolerating a "sinner".

Note: Many people assume that this sinful woman was Mary Magdalene but, although that is possible, it is an assumption that we cannot make. The differences between Luke's account and similar ones in Mark 14 v 1-11 and John 12 v 1-8 are not irreconcilable. However, we cannot be sure that they record the same event. It is also far from certain that the "Mary" mentioned in John 12 v 3 is Mary Magdalene. Finally, if this woman were Mary Magdalene, it is unlikely that she would be introduced as a new character in the passage that follows this account (see Luke 8 v 2). For these reasons, we will study this passage independently of the others.

GUIDANCE ON QUESTIONS

1. Imagine someone completely forgave you for doing something terribly wrong. How would it affect your relationship with that person? The purpose of this question is not only to encourage discussion, but also to highlight that gratitude and love are right responses to forgiveness.

2. Look back at Luke 7 v 29-30. What do we know about Pharisees? John preached "a baptism of repentance for the forgiveness of sins" (Luke 3 v 3). The Pharisee could well have been one of those mentioned in v 30, who rejected both John the Baptist and Jesus. It is interesting to note that the Pharisee would not have appeared to reject Jesus—after all, he had opened his home to Him!

3. Look at v 36-38. What do we learn about the woman? We are told that the woman had lived "a sinful life" in that town ie: her way of life was a public scandal. The fact that she comes to Jesus weeping, and anoints His feet with expensive perfume shows both that she is repentant, and that she turns to Jesus in her need.

⊗

- **In what ways is the behaviour of the Pharisee, and of the woman, surprising?** The religious person, the Pharisee, rejects Jesus; the "sinner" welcomes Him.

4. What does the Pharisee think about Jesus? Why does he think this? Simon assumes that Jesus doesn't know who the woman is or what she is like. As far as he

is concerned, it is the only explanation for the fact that Jesus, despite claiming to be sent from God (Luke 4 v 16-21), willingly accepts the attentions of this sinful woman. Contrary to popular belief (Luke 7 v 16-17), Simon then concludes that Jesus cannot be a prophet. What he doesn't realise is that not only does Jesus know exactly what kind of woman she is, but He also knows what Simon is thinking.

5. Use the table below to compare the Pharisee's actions with those of the woman.

The Pharisee	The woman
v 44: Doesn't give Jesus any water for washing feet.	**v 44:** Washes Jesus' feet with her tears.
v 45: Doesn't greet Jesus with a kiss.	**v 45:** Kisses Jesus' feet repeatedly.
v 46: Doesn't put any oil on Jesus' feet.	**v 46:** Pours expensive perfume on Jesus' feet

It is interesting to note that although providing water, welcoming with a kiss and anointing with olive oil were common practices, they were not required of a host. Jesus did not rebuke the Pharisee for being a bad host, but for his attitude toward Him (see Q6 below).

6. What do their actions show about their attitudes towards Jesus?

- **The Pharisee:** Although Simon had not been a bad host, there was nothing in his behaviour to suggest that he loved Jesus at all. His behaviour had been polite and correct, but that was all.

- **The woman:** This sinful woman clearly recognised Jesus as the forgiver of her sin. Her tears revealed her sorrow for sin and her gratitude for forgiveness. And her extravagant, self-sacrificial act of lavishing an expensive bottle of perfume on Jesus reflected an equally extravagant, self-sacrificial love. Jesus measured her love for Him by her actions toward Him—she "loved much".

7. Jesus tells a parable in v 40-42, which is explained in v 43-47. Who does the money-lender represent? Who do the two debtors represent? What does the parable mean? The money-lender: As the two men owed money to the money-lender, so we are in debt to God because of our sin. **The two debtors:** The man owing the greater debt represents the sinful woman; the man owing the lesser amount represents anyone who, in the Pharisee's estimation, is not too bad. This would have been his view of himself, although a wrong one.

The meaning of the parable: Jesus is not agreeing with this idea of greater and lesser sinfulness. He is demonstrating that, even according to Simon's view, the woman is to be commended for what she has done; she unashamedly shows her love and gratitude to the one who has forgiven her for so much—Jesus. Simon is confronted with Jesus' claim to be the one who can forgive sin, and is also compelled to think about his own lukewarm response to Jesus.

8. Why has the woman been forgiven (v 50)? Because of her faith (v 50). The term "faith" is misunderstood by many people, so at this point you should check that your group understands what faith is, and what (or who) she had faith in. The woman trusted that Jesus could forgive her sin (in contrast to the other guests—v 49). She was saved because she trusted Jesus to save her. It is also interesting to note that in the Old Testament, prophets, priests and kings were anointed. By anointing Jesus, it is possible

that she was acknowledging Him to be the ultimate Prophet, Priest and King (unlike Simon—v 39).

• **What did she have faith in?**

9. What does verse 47 mean? How might it be misunderstood? Verse 47 needs to be understood in the light of the rest of the passage. It seems to be saying that some Christians are forgiven more than others. But this is not consistent with the Bible's teaching on forgiveness. Every Christian is equally forgiven, but some may have a deeper understanding and appreciation of this forgiveness, which leads to a deeper love for Jesus.

Verse 47 also seems to suggest that the reason the woman was forgiven was because she loved Jesus. But this misunderstanding contradicts what the whole passage teaches—that love springs from forgiveness. The woman is not forgiven because she loved much; rather, the fact that she loved much is the evidence that she is forgiven. It is not the reason why she is forgiven but it is the reason why Jesus can say that she is forgiven.

If your group is struggling with this question, try asking these two:
• **Does v 47 mean that some Christians are forgiven more than others? If not, why not?**
• **Is v 47 saying that the woman was forgiven because she loved Jesus? If not, why not?**

To take the ideas raised in Q9 further, you might like to ask:
• **How can we tell that someone has**

been forgiven by God? Their lives will be marked by love and devotion to Jesus Christ.

- **How can we ourselves know that we have been forgiven by God?** We must be careful of basing our assurance of forgiveness on feelings alone—just because we feel unworthy of Christ's love, or worry that we don't love Him enough, it doesn't mean that we should doubt God's forgiveness. God forgives us on the basis of what Jesus Christ has done, not on the basis of how we feel. However, if we only feel indifference towards Christ, we should take that as an indication that we do not truly understand either our own sin, or God's forgiveness in Christ. How can we then say with certainty that we have been forgiven in Christ?

10. APPLY: The woman loved Jesus with a love that was considered excessive, and perhaps reckless or foolish—a lavish love pouring out a valuable perfume. Do we love Jesus the way this woman loved Him? What stops us? Sadly, unlike this woman, many Christians give very little of themselves to Jesus. This, according to Jesus, reveals very little love for Him and very little understanding or appreciation of His forgiveness. Many Christians don't go beyond the expectations of other Christians in their actions toward Jesus. Rather, in an attempt to avoid being called "extreme", as this woman was, they try to be as "normal" as possible. But this woman poured out an expensive bottle of perfume despite what others would say about her. Christians too should be motivated by love for Jesus, rather than a desire to fit in with other people. That passion should be reflected in the way we use our time, money, energy and conversations. Are we ever impulsive or

extravagant in showing our love for Jesus? The big thing that stops us from loving Jesus as this woman did is that we fail to truly understand our salvation: either the depth of our sin (the things that we have been forgiven), or the certainty of Jesus' full and free forgiveness (the fact that we have been totally forgiven). We may be like the Pharisee, convinced deep down that we don't really need Jesus. Or we may remain stuck in guilt and despair, only too aware of our sin, but unable to trust that Jesus has done everything necessary for our forgiveness. If we could truly understand what and how we have been forgiven, our love for and gratitude to Jesus would overrule other inhibitions, such as fear of what others may think or reluctance to draw attention to ourselves.

So the question is: why don't we understand the depth of our sin or the certainty of our forgiveness? This may be a good opportunity to challenge people to reflect personally on their answers to the following questions:

- **Do you know what the Bible says about how bad our sin is? Or about how wonderful Jesus' forgiveness is?**
- **Do you trust the teaching of the Bible? Or are you influenced by what other "voices" are saying?**
- **Have you asked God to open your eyes to His truth, so that it will impact your heart, your mind and your life?**

11. Look at verses 39 and 48-49. Simon and his guests are scandalised by what happens between Jesus and the woman. What do we learn about Simon and his guests from these verses? Jesus' host, Simon, was scandalised by Jesus' tolerance of the sinful woman (v 39). His guests were outraged at His claim to have forgiven her sin (their question in v 49 is laden with doubt and indignation).

• **What do we learn about Jesus?** Jesus' actions and words reveal His love for sinners and His authority to forgive sin. The answer to the question posed by the guests in v 49, contrary to what they thought, is "Jesus is God!"

☒

• **What was the Pharisee's attitude to "sinners"?** He did not count himself as one of them, and clearly considered that all right-thinking people should avoid any contact with them—v 39.

EXPLORE MORE
Read Luke 4 v 14-20, 7 v 20-22. What is the good news that Jesus brings? Who are the poor to whom He is preaching?
Luke introduces Jesus at the beginning of His public ministry, in Luke 4 v 14-30, as the anointed one from God who would preach good news to the poor, in fulfilment of the prophecy of Isaiah 61 v 1-2. Jesus claims this again in Luke 7 v 20-22. His encounter with this sinful woman reveals that the good news He preaches is forgiveness for sin—even the most obvious and shameful kind. The poor to whom He preaches this good news are those who understand that they have no goodness of their own, and no way of paying back their debt to God. This woman is an example of the "poor" whom the good news is for. She was considered by people like the Pharisees to be too sinful for salvation—too morally "poor" to claim the riches of heaven. And yet, in Luke 6 v 20

Jesus says: "Blessed are you who are poor, for yours is the kingdom of God".

12. APPLY: How can we be like the Pharisee in our attitude towards sinners? The Pharisee was self-righteous, proud, judgmental, critical, unforgiving, unloving and intolerant of "sinners"; he condemned the woman for her sin, but was not aware of his own sin and didn't recognise his own need for forgiveness. Although many of these character traits can be true of us too, they are often subtly disguised. If we think that God's forgiveness and love depend on how good or bad we are, it shows we have a self-righteous attitude. If we avoid people who we think are more sinful than us, it shows we have a proud and judgmental attitude.

☒

• **People don't usually admit to thinking like this, but what kind of things show that they have these attitudes?** For example: less interest in understanding key Christian teaching, such as the cross, but greater interest in laws and rules; annoyance when church changes to become more welcoming for non-Christians; little mention of Jesus Christ; etc.

• **If we come across someone who is obviously a sinner, how should we treat them? And how should we not treat them?** Discuss with your group which kind of responses betray the attitude of a Pharisee towards "sinners", and which show the love of Christ.

13. APPLY: Imagine you know someone who has deep and persistent guilt about past sins, which makes them doubt God's forgiveness and feel utterly unworthy of Christ's love. How can you use the things learned in this passage to help them? This question provides an opportunity to review the session and to check that the members of your group understand the basis on which we can receive forgiveness from God.

OPTIONAL EXTRA

Testimonies are the personal accounts of ordinary people about how God has worked in their lives. If people are willing to share, this may be a good opportunity to hear testimonies of how Christians first learned of God's forgiveness and the effect that this has had on them. Or you may prefer to share with your group a relevant passage from a Christian biography or autobiography.

4 Mark 5 v 24-34
FAITH THAT TRANSFORMS SUFFERING

THE BIG IDEA
We can have faith in Jesus' power over illness, suffering and death.

SUMMARY
Jesus displays His power over the law, uncleanness, illness and suffering. He does this by healing a woman who has been pronounced ceremonially unclean according to Jewish law, and by freeing her from her suffering. He does this in response to her extraordinary faith—she has lost faith in any human remedy, but she believes that even if she only touches Jesus, He will heal her. But Jesus is not content just to let her go on her way healed. He makes sure that she and everyone around knows that she has been healed, that it has happened because of His power, and that it has happened to this woman because she has shown faith in Jesus.

Note: The laws on ceremonial cleanness and uncleanness can be found in Leviticus.

The laws that applied to this woman's medical condition come from Leviticus 15 v 25-31. The woman's condition was one among many things that made people unfit to worship God at the tabernacle (later the temple in Jerusalem).

GUIDANCE ON QUESTIONS
1. Why do you think people react to suffering in such different ways? There can be many reactions to suffering that seem very different—questioning God's sovereignty or blaming Satan, giving in to despair and depression or struggling to overcome it in our own strength, or just trying to ignore suffering altogether. But actually, all these reactions have something in common—at the heart of each is an inability to reconcile the reality of suffering with the sovereignty and goodness of God. The only response that is fundamentally different is to trust God, whatever happens. This is something we can learn from the

example of other believers, such as the woman in this story. As we see Jesus demonstrate His authority and control over suffering, both in the lives of this woman and other Christians around us, we will be challenged to respond to suffering with faith.

2. How bad was this woman's situation? Read Leviticus 15 v 25-31. How does this help us to understand the depth of her suffering (v 25-26)? We know that this woman's situation was desperate from the fact that for 12 years every doctor she had visited had failed her. She had spent all her money on remedies that she hoped would make her better, yet now she was worse than ever. With no improvement and no money left, she must have felt desperate. But as if this were not bad enough, Leviticus 15 v 25-31 shows us that, under Jewish law, her medical condition made her ceremonially unclean (Leviticus 15 v 25). This meant she had to be separate from the Israelites and separate from God. For twelve years she had been banned from temple worship. She had also not been allowed to touch anyone else, since they too would become unclean through physical contact with her (Leviticus 15 v 31).

Notice that uncleanness was linked with sin, in that it separated the people from God and needed to be atoned for by offering sacrifices (Leviticus 15 v 29-30).

⊗

• **Why do you think the woman wanted to be anonymous (v 27-28)? Why was she so fearful of having to confess the truth publicly (v 33)?** It is likely that the whole crowd had been contaminated by her presence (see v 24, 31)! No wonder she trembled with fear as

she confessed the truth to Jesus—she had touched Him.

Note: Many interpret these laws to mean that God is unreasonably prejudiced against those groups of people who are pronounced unclean. If we have this view, it shows that we presume, equally unreasonably, that we are more loving and fair than God! You may need to spend some time helping your group understand the reason for these laws. We need to remember that the Old Testament is a huge visual aid of spiritual truths. We are told that God's eyes are "too pure to look on evil" (Habakkuk 1 v 13). This was represented visually to Israel (and now to us) by the fact that only healthy and whole people could worship God at the tabernacle/temple; in the same way, only perfect animals could be used for offerings to God. Make sure that people understand that these rules no longer apply to Christians. Christians have been made perfect forever by Jesus' sacrifice on the cross (Hebrews 10 v 14). As a result, all Christians are free to come to God at any time (Hebrews 10 v 19-22).

3. What is extraordinary about her healing (v 26-29)? Not only did Jesus do what medical doctors had failed to do, He did it without being contaminated by her touch.

• **What would normally be the result of this woman's physical contact with Jesus (see Leviticus 15 v 26-27)? What happens here, and what does that show us about Jesus?** Normally, Jesus would also become unclean through physical contact with this woman. However, what happened was that she was healed and became clean. By cleansing her, Jesus restored her to a relationship with God and fellowship with His people. He was able to do this because of the ultimate sacrifice of atonement that He would make when He died on the cross (see Hebrews 10 v 10-22).

4. What is remarkable about the woman's faith? Although this woman must have lost faith in the medical care of doctors, she had faith in Jesus' ability to heal her with just a touch. What reason did she have to believe that Jesus' touch would make her clean, rather than make Him unclean, if she did not believe that Jesus, being God, had authority to reverse the law? That is remarkable faith.

5. Look at v 30-34. Do you think that Jesus was aware of who had touched Him, and what His power had been used for (see also Luke 8 v 47)? Jesus certainly knew that someone had touched Him for the purpose of being helped by His power (v 30). From what we know of Jesus elsewhere, in particular His ability to know even what people were thinking, it seems likely that Jesus also knew who had touched Him. Luke 8 v 47 tells us that, despite the crowd, the woman knew that she could not go unnoticed.

6. What do you notice about how Jesus treats this woman? Jesus didn't expose the woman by pointing her out, but neither was He willing to let her slip away into the crowd unnoticed. He was compassionate in understanding her weakness and fear, yet also resolute in wanting her to publicly confess her own faith and His power.

- **Why do you think that He brings her to public attention (v 32-34)?** There are a number of reasons why Jesus could have wanted to speak to her publicly: so that He

could announce to everyone that she was now "clean"; so that He could establish a relationship with her; so that she would confess what Jesus had done for her; so that everyone listening would know of His power; so that He could give her assurance and encourage her in her new-found faith (v 34).

- **What does the woman want from Jesus?** To be freed from her suffering.
- **What does Jesus want?** He wants her to be freed from her suffering, but He also wants her to meet Him, to receive assurance and blessing from Him, and for everyone around to know what has happened in the life of this woman and why.

7. APPLY: Jesus not only wants us to put our faith in Him; He wants our faith in Him to be seen by others. How would you use this passage to help someone who is a secret believer in Jesus? Use the points raised in Q6 to discuss why we need to be public followers of Jesus, rather than secret believers. Notice that the reasons given involve both greater blessing for us, and our responsibility to be witnesses of Jesus Christ in this world.

Note: At this point, some may raise the difficulties facing believers, especially women, who have converted to Christianity from a Muslim background. Since Islam decrees that any Muslim who converts to another religion should be killed, it is likely that there are many secret believers throughout Islamic nations. Jesus clearly teaches that His followers must be prepared to die for following Him (see Mark 8 v 34-35; Luke 14 v 26-27). However, we would do well not to judge these hard-pressed fellow believers when we do not face such pressures ourselves. It would be more relevant to steer the discussion back to the reasons why some still want to be secret believers when there is no threat to life.

8. Why has the woman been healed (v 34)? In what way could verse 34 be misunderstood? Jesus tells the woman that she has been healed because of her faith. It is easy to misunderstand verse 34 because it seems to suggest that the woman was able to claim Jesus' healing power with her faith. This is a popular idea in churches today. But it is a dangerous idea because it assumes that the power to heal lies within us (our faith), rather than with Jesus, as this passage clearly explains (v 30). By saying, "your faith has healed you", Jesus did not mean that her faith healed her, but that, because of her faith, He had healed her.

- **What did this woman have faith in?** She had faith in Jesus' ability to heal her, rather than faith in her own faith. Her faith was the channel, but it was Jesus' power that did the work of healing.
- **What should we have faith in?** We should have faith in Jesus' power to forgive our sin, change us and raise us from death to eternal life.
- **What should we not have faith in?** We should not have faith in anything we do or are, including our faith. Our only hope of being forgiven, changed, resurrected and welcomed into eternal life is what Jesus has done in dying for us on the cross.

9. Over what things does Jesus display His power?

• From what things does Jesus free this woman?

Jesus displays His authority and power over the law, over illness, over uncleanness and over suffering.

EXPLORE MORE
From Mark 5 v 21-23 and 35-43, what are the similarities and differences between the two stories? *Similarities*: A common theme in both of these stories is faith. Both the woman and Jairus believe in Jesus' ability to heal with just a touch (v 23, 28), and in both stories Jesus addresses their faith—He commends the woman for hers (v 34) and challenges Jairus in his (v 36). Also, in both stories Jesus displays His unique power to heal through a miracle. Notice also the similar linking phrase "fell at His feet" (v 22, 33).
Differences: There are differences between the two characters: one is a synagogue ruler, the other an unclean woman. Their social status could not have been further apart, but they are equal before Jesus.
What else do we learn about Jesus' power? Jairus believed Jesus could *prevent* death (v 23), but Jesus showed He could *reverse* death. Jairus' daughter was clearly dead. The people were certain of this: they were "crying and wailing loudly" (v 38). The suggestion that she was only sleeping prompted disdainful laughter (v 40). But Jesus did not mean she was asleep, but that He would raise her from the dead as easily as they might wake her up every morning.
In what ways do these two miracles foreshadow Jesus' death and resurrection? Jesus demonstrated His ultimate authority and power over death through His own death and resurrection.

Death had no power over Him. Also, the reason why Jesus was able to heal the woman of her illness and cleanse her of her uncleanness, was because, through His death on the cross, He would offer Himself as the atoning sacrifice for her uncleanness (see Leviticus 15 v 29-30, Romans 3 v 23-25).

10. APPLY: What has struck you about how this woman responds to her suffering? The woman was bold in approaching Jesus—she must have known the prohibition on touching other people, yet she seemed to trust that all of that would be overcome if she could only receive the healing power of Jesus; she was so confident of the greatness of His power that she was content simply to touch His clothes; she was persistent—the presence of the crowd would not have made it easy to get close to Jesus, but she followed Him until she was able to touch His garment; she was humble, not wanting to draw attention to herself or take up Jesus' time; she was submissive—when she realised that Jesus wanted her to come out into the open, she complied.

• **Imagine you face a difficult situation this week. Think of a particular way that you can put into practice what you have learned from this passage.** Discuss how the points listed above would make a practical difference in a difficult situation. You may want to think of some examples of difficult situations for people to discuss eg: a diagnosis of cancer in the family; the threat of being sacked for not following orders that go against your conscience.

11. APPLY: Some people say that if you have enough faith, you will be healed.

How would you respond to that? This comment shows that someone's confidence is in faith, rather than in the Lord. Since Jesus is Lord, we must accept that He may not want us to be healed of a particular sickness. We should be convinced that He can heal us, but we don't know if He will heal us. During His earthly ministry, Jesus healed people to prove His claim to be the Christ. This means that the woman could be confident of instant healing as she approached Christ, in a way that we can't today. We, however, can be utterly confident of Jesus' power to forgive our sin, change us and raise us from death to eternal life. And confident that through all the hardships that we face, God is sovereign and good, and is working out His good purposes for us (see Explore More below).

EXPLORE MORE
What reasons do [James 4 v 3; John 14 v 13-14, 15 v 7-8; Matthew 7 v 7-11; Romans 8 v 28-29] give us why God does not always respond to our prayers in the way in which we would like?
You might want to split your group up into pairs or threes, each looking at one or two of these passages.

Although Jesus does not always heal in response to faith as He did during His earthly ministry, He still has the power to do so and He still responds to prayers of faith. However, He does not always respond in the way in which we would like. Here are some reasons why not:

James 4 v 3: Our wrong (selfish) motives are often the reason why God does not give us what we ask for.

John 14 v 13-14; 15 v 7-8: Jesus only promises to answer prayers that are in line with His character, word and will ("in my name"—His name represents who He is), and which bring glory to God.

Matthew 7 v 7-11; Romans 8 v 28-29:
God will only give us "good gifts". If what we ask for isn't good for us (if it won't make us more like His Son—Romans 8 v 29), He won't give it to us.

• **How could you use these verses to help someone in the difficult situation that you discussed in Q10?**

OPTIONAL EXTRA

The newspapers are full of reports of death and illness and tragedy. Read a recent newspaper article together and spend some time discussing how Christians ought to respond to that tragedy, bearing in mind what you have learned this session.

---

5 Matthew 15 v 21 – 28
FAITH THAT PERSEVERES

THE BIG IDEA

The Canaanite woman shows that great faith in the mercy of God, brought to all people through the Lord Jesus, produces perseverance.

SUMMARY

The Canaanite woman came to Jesus knowing that she was unworthy. She was a Canaanite, a member of a pagan race who had always been considered enemies of Israel. But she also believed that Jesus is the King, who will bring blessing to all nations, and that He would always have a crumb of mercy to spare. She trusted in the Lord's abundant mercy, and this was what drove her to persevere in seeking help from Jesus, even when she did not receive an immediate answer to her need. Jesus never intended to discourage her, but rather, to test and reward her faith. Ultimately, His intention was always to grant her request.

At the same time, He was showing His disciples that, although His own ministry focused on Israel, the blessings of His gospel are for all people. Jesus' surprising and strange conversation with this woman revealed to the disciples exactly who He had come to save (Jews first, but then Gentiles as well) and how (it's all and only through faith in Him). When the woman's faith rose to the test, Jesus responded by answering her need. When the disciples saw this encounter, they learned that a non-Jew could hear Jesus and respond with greater faith than many Jews.

Note: In Old Testament times, the Canaanites were one of the races that had lived in the territory promised by God to Israel (Exodus 3 v 8). God commanded Israel to completely destroy them (Deuteronomy 20 v 17). However, Israel failed to do this (Judges 1 v 28). Canaanites continued to live in and around the land of Israel, and, as this story shows, were still doing so at the time of Jesus. Because of their paganism, they were considered detestable by the Jews.

The Canaanite woman's faith shines brighter against the dark backdrop of Matthew 15 v 1-20. While the Pharisees judge Jesus and

His disciples, the Canaanite woman pleads for mercy. While the religious elite reject Jesus, this pagan woman seeks Him.

The Pharisees have accused Jesus' disciples of breaking their traditions and of eating with unclean hands. Jesus explains that it is obedience to God's word that matters, not human traditions. It is the condition of their hearts that makes them unclean, rather than religious rituals (or lack of them). Jesus redefines what it means to be unclean. He then shows His rejection of the Pharisees' teaching, by moving on into territory that the Pharisees would consider unclean (the region of Tyre and Sidon—v 21), and meeting with a woman that they would have utterly despised because of her racial origins.

GUIDANCE ON QUESTIONS

1. Think of something in your life that you wanted to do and tried to do, but eventually gave up. Why didn't you persevere? The purpose of this question is to encourage the group to discuss one of the key subjects of this study—perseverance.

2. What is surprising in verse 22? Because this woman is a Canaanite, it is astonishing that she addresses Jesus as: "Lord, Son of David" (v 22). To address Jesus like this shows that she is familiar with God's promises to His people. God had promised that King David would have a son who would rule forever (2 Samuel 7 v 12-16). The woman is acknowledging that Jesus is this King—her King. She, a Canaanite, wants to be included in God's promised kingdom!

3. What do the woman's words in verse 22 show us about:
• **her understanding of Jesus?** She acknowledges Jesus as her King. She

clearly understands that His rule extends beyond the borders of Israel, for she believes that He is her King. She also understands that He has authority over evil spirits, for she believes that He can release her daughter from demon-possession. She believes that Jesus is King over the physical world and King over the spiritual world! Finally, she trusts that Christ will be merciful.

• **her view of herself?** She begs "have mercy on me" (v 22) because she realises that she doesn't deserve anything from Jesus.

4. What has driven her to cry out to Jesus? Her daughter's suffering.

5. APPLY: What can we learn from this encounter about how God uses suffering for our good? Often it takes pain and anguish to drive us to God. Suffering like this makes us aware of our own weakness and of our need for God's help and comfort. No wonder God allows suffering! This woman is one example among many of how God uses evil for good. If her daughter had not been demon-possessed, she may not have come to Jesus. And if she had not come to Jesus, she would not have found the mercy and help that only He could give.

• **Do you have an example like this of the way in which suffering drove you to the Lord? What was the effect on your life?** Allow people to briefly share from their own experiences, as this can be so encouraging for others, but don't let this discussion distract you from the Bible study.

6. How do the disciples react to the woman's desperate request? "Send her away, for she keeps crying out after us" (v 23). Despite her desperate situation, the disciples feel no compassion for her. Their concern is not for her, but for themselves—their peace and quiet. They just want to get rid of her. Apparently, they shared the commonly-held Jewish view of a Canaanite, and did not think that she was worthy of help from the Lord. Maybe they interpreted Jesus' silence as disapproval of this woman. Certainly they had not yet understood that Jesus had come to save the whole world, and not just the Jews.

It may be worthwhile discussing how much like the disciples we can be. For instance, have we ever avoided helping people in need, basically because doing so would be inconvenient? Are our comforts more important to us than the salvation of other people?

7. Why do you think that Jesus doesn't answer her at first (v 23a)?

⌄

- **In what ways could the woman have responded to Jesus' silence?**
- **How do you think Jesus wanted the woman to respond?**
- **What would make the difference between responding with perseverance and giving up?**

Jesus wants to test this woman's faith and put it on display in front of His disciples. His silence doesn't mean "no" or "yes"; it means "wait". Having to wait requires patience and perseverance. And whether or not we persevere shows whether or not we really trust Jesus. Faith motivates us to persevere. Without it, we give up. So if God's silence tests our faith, then perseverance will show that we have passed the test.

8. How does she respond to this test (v 25)? What does her response show about her view of Jesus? She keeps asking: "Lord, help me!" Her perseverance proves that she trusts Jesus. If she had doubted that Jesus would have mercy on her, why would she have kept asking? He had tested her and she had passed with flying colours.

9. Jesus' words in v 24 and 26 sound harsh. What does He mean by them? "Words cannot convey a twinkle in the eye" (R.T. France). Jesus' words sound harsh, but that doesn't mean that His tone and expression were harsh as well. From what we have learned in previous sessions, we can be confident that, even though provocative and challenging, Jesus would have been loving towards this woman.

- **verse 24 (see Matthew 10 v 5-6):** At this stage, Jesus' mission focused on the Jews. The Canaanite woman, as a Gentile (non-Jew), was outside the focus of Jesus' ministry. In Matthew 10 v 5-6 Jesus had sent out the twelve disciples with these instructions: "Do not go among the Gentiles or enter any town of the Samaritans. Go rather to the lost sheep of Israel". Jesus was, first of all, Israel's Messiah—the promised King sent by God to rescue His people. But this didn't mean that Gentiles were excluded from Jesus' mission. In the Old Testament, Isaiah had prophesied that the Messiah would "restore the tribes of Jacob", but then also be "light for the Gentiles" (non-Jews) (Isaiah 49 v 6). After Jesus' death and resurrection—after the Jews had rejected Him by nailing Him to a cross—Jesus announced that His ministry would extend to other nations (Matthew 28 v 19). This story is a foretaste of what was to come. But Jesus was saying more than this. By having mercy on this Canaanite woman, He was including her in "the lost sheep of Israel". The term no longer refers to the Jews, but to all who come to Jesus for mercy!

- **verse 26:** Jews often referred to Gentiles as "dogs" (unclean animals). The Greek word (kynarion), used here by both Jesus and the woman, means pup or pet and is more affectionate than the derogatory word for an unkempt stray. Jesus was not using the term as an insult, but as a challenge. He is saying: "It is not right to take what belongs to the Jews and toss it to the Gentiles". And the unspoken question which follows is: "True or false?" He is testing her to see how she will respond. Will she doubt or will her faith rise to the challenge?

10. In verse 28 Jesus praises this woman for her faith. How does her answer show faith in Jesus? Undeterred by Jesus' answers, the woman responds by saying: "True, but false!" She agrees with Jesus, but argues that Jesus always has a crumb of mercy to spare—and just a crumb of His mercy will be more than enough. Her humility is astounding! She doesn't defend herself. She doesn't accuse Jesus of racism or discrimination, as we might. She knows that she is unworthy of His mercy, but she also knows that He is merciful—and that His mercy is bountiful and overflowing!

- **What is remarkable about her faith?** Put yourself in her shoes. You, the arch-enemy of the Jews, have come to their King for help. His followers just want to be rid of you. The King at first says nothing.

When He finally does speak, His words are difficult to accept. And yet you press on. This woman could have felt that she was being ignored and discouraged, but instead, she never doubted that Jesus had overflowing mercy and power—not only enough for all the "lost sheep of Israel", but for herself and her daughter as well.

- **What have the disciples learned by seeing her faith?** The disciples learn that although Jesus' priority is to preach the good news to Israel, that doesn't mean exclusively to Israel. God's mercy is so abundant that there is plenty for non-Jews as well. Racial origin is irrelevant when it comes to faith—this woman was a pagan, but Jesus commends her for her "great faith", which stands in stark contrast to the hypocrisy of the Pharisees (v 7) and the dullness of the disciples (v 16).

11. APPLY: What have you learned from the Canaanite woman? How can we follow her example? This is an opportunity for the group to review and share things that have particularly struck and challenged them. Here are some points worth emphasising: the woman's great understanding of who Jesus was (v 22)—far greater than that of the Jewish religious leaders, or even the disciples; the woman's humility—she never responds with indignation, and she keeps asking for mercy; the woman's remarkable faith, which results in perseverance; the woman's positive response to Jesus' mini-parable (v 26-27)—she doesn't simply react, but listens carefully and answers Jesus by extending the parable.

12. APPLY: How do you respond when God doesn't seem to be listening to your prayer requests? When God doesn't seem to answer our prayers, often doubt creeps into our minds. We begin to question His love for us, or His sovereignty over the situation. Has He heard? Does He care? As a result, we are discouraged from asking for God's help. Instead, we take matters into our own hands. And the reason we do this is because we lack faith in both Jesus' willingness and ability to help us.

- **How can this passage help you to persevere in prayer?** We need to remind ourselves again of the character of God. He is merciful—abundantly so. There is always a crumb to spare for those who come to Him in faith. To understand and trust God like this, we need to know His history and His promises, as this woman did. We must stop sitting in judgment on God ("If I were God, I would have done X, Y and Z by now"); instead, we should come, like the woman, recognising that we deserve nothing and asking only for His mercy.

⊠

- **What can we do practically to help one another trust God's mercy, as this woman did?** Share ideas that people can put into practice. Some may find the words of Christian songs helpful in reminding themselves of God's abundant mercy eg: "The steadfast love of the Lord never ceases. His mercies never come to an end. They are new every morning, new every morning. Great is your faithfulness, O Lord. Great is your faithfulness."

EXPLORE MORE
Read Luke 18 v 1-8. Why should we "always pray and not give up" (v 1)? How can people misunderstand this parable? How does the example of the Canaanite woman's faith help us to

understand the parable correctly?
Is a judge who doesn't fear God or love others—a judge who has no concern for justice—likely to help a widow with no social standing and no money? No! And yet, because she persistently asks for justice, he does help her! Is the God of love and justice likely to help us when we cry to Him for help? Yes! If an unjust judge responds to the nagging of a widow, the just God will certainly answer the persistent prayers of His chosen ones!

People misunderstand this parable by equating God with the character of the unjust judge! It shows how easily we can adopt the attitude of the world, in doubting the fundamental goodness of God's character. Surely the Canaanite woman would have got the point of the parable straightaway—if it is worthwhile pestering an unjust judge for help, it is infinitely more worthwhile to persevere in prayer to a just and merciful God.

OPTIONAL EXTRA
Some of the people in your group may find it very difficult to come to terms with Jesus' silence and strong words in this passage. If you have access to a television and DVD player, it may be helpful to watch a scene from the film *Ray*—a biopic of the singer Ray Charles. Seven-year-old Ray, having recently lost his sight, trips while running into the house. Despite his earnest cries for help, his mother says and does nothing, tears streaming down her face. Why? She wants her son to be strong and overcome difficulties himself. The illustration is not perfect (God tests us to strengthen our faith in Him, not our ability to cope without Him), but it does show us that it is sometimes kind to be "cruel", as in this passage.

6 Luke 10 v 38-42
FAITH THAT LISTENS TO JESUS

THE BIG IDEA

Spending time with the Lord by listening to His word is more important than anything else—even than serving Him.

SUMMARY

While Mary hung on Jesus' every word, Martha busied herself in the kitchen and fretted over the meal. Mary listened: Martha served. And Jesus said that what Mary had chosen was better. Why? Because our greatest need is to know Jesus—to be in a relationship with Him. But we can't know Him unless we listen to Him, because that is how He reveals Himself to us. Serving Jesus is important, but not as important as spending time with Him. In fact, Christian service can often distract us from reading, listening to, learning from and reflecting upon God's word, as it did Martha.

Note: In Luke 10 v 25-28 Jesus confirmed that the expert in the law was right when he said the way to inherit eternal life was to "Love the Lord your God with all your heart..." and "Love your neighbour as yourself". The parable of the Good Samaritan shows what it means to "love your neighbour". The story of Martha and Mary shows us what it means to "love the Lord your God"—attaching yourself to Jesus and devoting yourself to His teaching. Mary is an example of a woman who loved and adored Jesus with all her heart.

GUIDANCE ON QUESTIONS

1. What things do you make time to do each day, no matter how busy you are? Why do you make those things a priority? The aim of this question is to get the group thinking and talking about what our highest priorities are. We make time for the things that we need to do, such as sleeping, eating, working and looking after our children. And we make time for the things that we enjoy doing, such as watching a movie, reading a novel or meeting a friend for coffee.

2. What can we learn from Martha from verse 38? Martha "opened her home" to Jesus (v 38). She clearly welcomed and respected Jesus.

3. What can we learn about Mary from verse 39? See also John 11 v 1-2, 32 and 12 v 1-7. These references paint a beautiful portrait of Mary.
First, Mary is humble. There are three accounts of Martha and Mary in the New Testament and in each of these we find Mary at Jesus' feet. She "sat at the Lord's feet" in Luke 10 v 39, she "fell at His feet" in John 11 v 32 and she poured expensive perfume on His feet in John 12 v 3. This humble position was where she felt most comfortable.
Second, she is quiet and attentive to Jesus. In all three accounts mentioned above, Mary says only 12 words (see John 11 v 32). We see Mary "listening" intently (v 39). Jesus explained to His disciples many times that He would die in Jerusalem, but His death came as a surprise to them. But Mary

poured perfume on Jesus in preparation for His burial (John 12 v 7). Did Mary know Jesus would die? If so, was it because she listened?

4. What did Martha get wrong? Martha's hospitality distracted her from listening to Jesus (v 40). Her priorities were wrong.

- **What do you think were the "many things" (v 41) that Martha was worried about?** Martha was worried about "all the preparations that had to be made"—the cooking, the baking, the cleaning, the presentation etc. Like Martha, many women worry about meeting the expectations of others and end up trying to be the perfect housewife or hostess.

- **What was the "one" thing (v 42) that she needed to be concerned about?** Ultimately, none of the things that worried Martha mattered. But taking this unique and limited opportunity to spend time with Jesus—that mattered. She didn't need to be the perfect hostess. She needed to hear what Jesus had to say.

5. APPLY: How can we listen to Jesus now? Jesus' words are recorded for us in the Bible. We can listen to Jesus by hearing God's word taught and explained by others, as well as reading, studying, memorising and meditating on it ourselves. When we spend time in God's word, we should be expecting to grow in our relationship with Him—to know Him more. We mustn't treat the Bible like an academic textbook, but like a letter—it is God's word to us!

- **Why is it so important to make spending time in God's word our greatest concern?** God has revealed Himself to us through His word. It is only through His word that we can know God

through Jesus.
- The Bible protects us. This world bombards us with its values and ideas, all of which oppose God. We are constantly being moulded and pressured to live according to the ways of the world. It is vital that we read God's word so that we can arm ourselves against these influences.
- The Bible is our guide to a truly successful life ie: living to please our sovereign creator God and being part of His purposes in this world. 2 Timothy 3 v 16-17 tells us that the Bible equips us "for every good work". Spending time in God's word will help us to be more Christ-like in the way we think, speak and live.

- **Do you think that you really realise how important God's word is?**

6. APPLY: How do we get distracted from listening to Jesus? What kind of things do we worry about? The list of distractions is different for each one of us, but endless for all of us. Life in the 21st century demands more time than we seem to have. We worry about our futures, our decisions, our money, our jobs, our relationships and our loved ones, until we are too worn out or too absorbed in our concerns to find comfort and help from God's word. Many are pressured to work long hours. Others need to care for family and friends. By contrast, some have plenty of free time but get sucked into watching TV or reading magazines, obsessively following hobbies, health and fitness or celebrity gossip. According to Jesus, all these things are just "distractions" if spending time with Him is not our highest priority. They distract us from the one thing that we really need: to listen to what He has to say.

- **What can we do to make sure that our time of reading and reflecting on God's word doesn't get squeezed out by other things?** Why not revisit your answers to Q1 at this point? There are a couple of useful questions to ask about these "priorities"? Eg: Is this a matter of responsibility or of enjoyment? What would happen if this particular priority was missed out—who would be affected, and would it really matter?

Note: For many Christians, one of the biggest distractions can be church commitments. Of course, it is good for all Christians to be involved in Christian service. But if we have no time left to spend with the Lord, it is rather like a parent who looks after a child but never speaks to it—the lack of relationship makes the parent's activity pointless. For tips on how to know when Christian service has become more important than our relationship with the Lord, see Q11.

- **Why not share some practical ideas that could help us to be more effective in listening to Jesus through God's word?** Eg: Susannah Wesley would put an apron over her head so that she could pray even when she was looking after her umpteen children; one young mother used times her children were watching TV to read the Bible; take notes during Bible teaching and make time to look at them later; meet, phone or email someone during the week to discuss and pray about Bible teaching you have heard or a passage you have read etc.

EXPLORE MORE

Read Acts 6 v 1-4. What was the highest priority for the apostles in the first days of the church? Why do you think this was so important? How should this priority be reflected in our churches today? "It would not be right for us to neglect the ministry of the word of God in order to wait on tables" (Acts 6 v 2). Mercy ministries—in this case providing for widows—are important, but "word" ministry is vital. Preaching God's word is a higher priority than serving food, because food sustains life on earth, but the word of God gives eternal life—and brings us into relationship with Jesus.

A good church will reflect the principle that the ministry of the word of God (including prayer—Acts 6 v 4) should never be neglected. Here are some helpful questions to ask about a church: Is teaching the Bible central to all groups and ages in the church, from children's clubs to senior citizens, including services, home-groups, evangelism, etc? What importance is given to prayer in meetings and to prayer meetings? How much of a priority is it to find, set apart, train and send out those who are gifted in Bible-teaching?

7. Compare the two women. What do you find most striking?

- **What do Martha's words in v 40 reveal about her attitude to...**
  - **her sister?**
  - **Jesus?**
- **What do Mary's lack of words tell us?**

Mary is quiet and attentive while Martha is careless with her words. She has not yet realised that she is the one who needs to be rebuked (v 41-42). She reproaches Mary: "my sister has left me to do the work by myself", and even Jesus: "Lord, don't you care…?" What a thoughtless thing to say! She is so upset that her emotions get the better of her mind and her tongue! But perhaps the most astounding thing she says is yet to come: "Tell her to help me!" (v 40). While Mary quietly listens to what Jesus has to say, Martha interrupts Him and tells Him what to say! Mary, on the other hand, doesn't try to defend herself or get drawn into an argument. She is content to let Jesus handle the situation.

8. Why does Jesus commend Mary's listening rather than Martha's service?

"Mary has chosen what is better" (v 42). According to Jesus, it is better to listen to Him than to serve Him. Here are a few reasons why Jesus made that point:

- God has more to do in you than through you! Christianity is about what God can do for you, not about what you can do for Him. It is about grace, not works. Our relationship with Jesus should demonstrate that. Mary's did: she wanted to receive. Martha's didn't: she wanted to give.
- Jesus has the words of eternal life (John 6 v 68). We must listen to Jesus because He is the one who holds the key to eternity. If we don't spend time listening to Him, our "service" may end up counting for nothing (Matthew 7 v 21-23).
- In Matthew 6 v 25-34 Jesus reassures us that we do not need to worry about practical things if we seek His kingdom first.
- Listening to Jesus will never distract us from serving Him—it will encourage us to! But service can distract us from listening. It can replace Jesus as the centre of our attention.
- Our relationship with Jesus should be personal as well as functional. Mary's relationship with the Lord was beautiful because it was close and intimate. She spent time with Jesus. She listened to Jesus. She knew Jesus.

9. How does Jesus deal with the two women?

Jesus deals with Martha firmly, but gently. He is uncompromising, but gracious. He understands that she is worried and upset, but maintains that she is wrong.

10. APPLY: Why do you think women like Mary are so rare?

Mary was utterly devoted to Jesus, her Saviour and Lord. Her aim was to be with Him and learn from Him while she had the opportunity. This meant that she was unconcerned about lesser things such as social customs, or the expectations of others, like Martha. There are no simple answers to the question of why we do not often see this kind of single-minded devotion to the Lord. It may be a lack of understanding of God's truth about our sin and the gospel; it may be that we have never asked God to fill our hearts with love for Jesus, because we are too self-reliant; it may be that we enjoy worldly pleasures too much to seek enjoyment in our relationship with Jesus; etc. What is clear is that it was Mary's single-minded devotion to the Lord that shaped her character and her behaviour. We can only be like her if we have the same love and appreciation for Jesus.

- **What is it about Mary that safeguards her from charges of laziness or slackness in hospitality?** Whatever Martha may have thought, we know that Mary was not guilty of being lazy or slack about hospitality, because of the way in which Jesus commended her for doing something better than serving Him. Of course, Christians may sometimes opt out of service because they are lazy—the key difference is that they are only interested in pleasing themselves, whereas the most important thing for Mary was to please her Lord.

11. APPLY: It is good to serve Christ; but how can we know whether our serving has become more important to us than listening to Him? Here are some tell-tale signs that serving has become more important than spending time with the Lord:

- If you know in your heart of hearts that you would rather work than pray and read or listen to God's word.
- If you would rather sacrifice your time with the Lord than your ministry.
- If you serve in church at the cost of your own relationship with Jesus (ie: you miss teaching and prayer because of your ministry—eg: teaching Sunday school—but you never try to make up for it eg: listen to Bible teaching on CD etc).
- If you continually feel the need to tell others about your work for God.

7 John 11 v 1-44
FAITH THAT OVERCOMES DEATH

THE BIG IDEA
Jesus understands the overwhelming power and devastation of death and yet, calmly and in His own time, displays total power and control over this greatest enemy; if we don't trust Jesus as Martha and Mary did, we have no hope in the face of death.

SUMMARY
This passage is a bold proclamation of the fact that Jesus is the only hope in the face of death to be found in the entire universe. Jesus presents this astounding truth in a dramatic way. Everything seems arranged to make it as difficult as possible for Jesus to carry off His final and greatest miracle—the decomposition of a four-day-old corpse; the desolation of Martha and Mary, who love Him; the doubt of the Jews, who openly question whether Jesus really has the power

of God that He claims, or whether He truly loved Lazarus; and the backdrop of the disciples' horror, and then resignation, at Jesus' apparently suicidal determination to go to Jerusalem. But then the moment arrives for Jesus to finally be proved right or wrong in His 'unbelievable' claim to be the resurrection and the life. It takes just three ordinary words from Jesus to bring Lazarus immediately back to active, healthy life. Jesus can raise the dead as simply as waking a sleeping child.

Jesus delayed going to Bethany so that no one would doubt that Lazarus was dead and therefore, that He had raised him from the dead. He did this to prove that He has the power to give life—eternal life. The death of their brother caused Martha and Mary a great deal of pain, but unlike the Jews, they never questioned Jesus' power or love. They didn't know the reason why He had allowed Lazarus to die—it was so that many more would believe and live—but they trusted Him nevertheless.

Note: At this point, Jesus' own death and resurrection are looming (v 8, 16). In raising Lazarus from the dead, Jesus is previewing to His disciples His own resurrection.

GUIDANCE ON QUESTIONS

1. All of us at some stage have experienced (or will) the death of a loved one. How do different people deal with the shock and pain involved? How can we prepare ourselves for this experience? The purpose of this question is to examine how we respond to death, and perhaps to show people that there is little we can do to prepare positively for bereavement. People need to understand the depth of human hopelessness in the face of death, in order to appreciate truly the wonderful hope that can only be found in Christ.

2. How did Jesus feel about Lazarus and his sisters (verses 3 and 5, see also verse 36)? Jesus loved Lazarus. Martha and Mary knew that He did (v 3). John, one of Jesus' disciples and the writer of this account, believed that He loved this family (v 5). And even the Jews had to admit that Jesus loved Lazarus when they saw Him weeping after Lazarus' death (v 36).

3. Why did Jesus delay going to Bethany to see Lazarus (v 6)? After four days, Lazarus' body would have begun to decompose (v 39). Jesus wanted to ensure that there would be no room for doubt that Lazarus was dead, and therefore no possibility of questioning whether Jesus had really raised him from the dead. And He had planned it this way for two reasons:

- **verse 4:** "For God's glory so that God's Son may be glorified through it" (v 4). It is important to note that God is glorified when His Son, Jesus, is glorified. We will look at what this means in more detail under Q14.

- **verses 11-15:** So that His people would believe in Him (v 14-15). In John 20 v 30-31, John tells us the purpose of Jesus' miracles: "These are written that you may believe that Jesus is the Messiah, the Son of God, and that by believing you may have life in his name". This miracle is no exception. Jesus claimed that He was in control of His own death (v 9-10), but His disciples didn't believe Him (v 16). He had planned to raise Lazarus from the dead to prove that He had authority over death— even His own—"so that you may believe" (v 14-15). And in John 12 v 10-11 we read that "many of the Jews were going over to Jesus and believing in him" because of Lazarus' resurrection.

4. How did Martha and Mary handle their brother's death (v 20-22, 32)? The way these sisters clung to and trusted Jesus is truly heart-warming. It may seem as though Mary's grief was deeper than Martha's. Mary stayed at home, presumably too overcome with sorrow to leave the house. And she wept at Jesus' feet (v 33); no mention is made of Martha's tears, however. But we must remember that the two sisters had very different personalities. We saw in the last session that Mary was quieter and more reflective. They handled their grief differently.

Although there are differences between Martha and Mary, they had one thing in common: they responded to the death of their brother by going to Jesus (v 20, 28-29).

Their first words to Jesus were identical (v 21, 32). Both regretted that Jesus had not been there. They were not blaming or questioning Jesus. Rather, they were expressing their faith in His ability to have prevented Lazarus' death. But that is where their faith ended. Had they believed that Jesus could reverse death, they would have had no reason to regret His absence.

5. What was Martha's hope (v 22-24)? Compare verse 39.

Martha believed that at the last day, Lazarus would be raised to life, but that wasn't the same as believing that Jesus could and would raise Lazarus to life there and then. Some people think that Martha did believe that Jesus could reverse death, because of her words in v 22 ("God will give you whatever you ask"). That is what she seems to believe (v 36). But... (see follow-up question below):

⌄

• **Compare Martha's words in v 22 with her response to Jesus' instruction in v 39. What does this show us about Martha's belief?** Her statement in v 22 is no more than mere words. Her protest in v 39 betrays her: "But, Lord ... by this time there is a bad odour, for he has been there four days". Often, what we say we believe doesn't stand up to the test. It is more likely that what she was saying in verse 22 is this: "But I know that even now, God will raise Lazarus on the last day if you ask Him to". This would make sense of the conversation that followed. Martha's hope was that God would give her brother eternal life. And what a great hope it was! But not as great as it would be when she truly understood who Jesus was.

• **In eternity, what will Lazarus, Martha and Mary be more thankful for—the resurrection at Bethany, or the resurrection at the last day?** However grateful they will be for the miracle at Bethany, Lazarus, Martha and Mary will certainly be most thankful for their resurrection to eternal life at the last day. The purpose of this question is to help people understand that, despite the wonder of Jesus' miracle in raising Lazarus back to life in this world, it was only ever a preview of something greater and far more wonderful—the truth that those in Christ will be raised for ever at the last day.

6. What did Jesus explain to Martha in verses 25-26?

Jesus explains to Martha the reason why she can have the hope of eternal life—because He is the "resurrection and the life" (v 25). This means that Jesus can resurrect people and give them new life (not merely preserve their old life, as Martha thought). He is the source of the eternal life she hopes for! And He gives eternal life to those who believe. He proved this by raising Lazarus from the dead. We can have no hope of eternal life without Jesus.

7. In v 26 Jesus asked Martha: "Do you believe this?" How did Martha respond? What does this show us about true belief?

In v 27 Martha responds by stating what she believes about Jesus: "Yes, Lord ... I believe that you are the Messiah, the Son of God, who is to come into the world". Martha believed that Jesus could give eternal life because she knew who He was. But she not only knew who He was—she had already shown how she trustingly submitted to Him as Lord of her life. To receive eternal life we need to believe in Jesus. And believing in Jesus means acknowledging that

He is the promised Saviour-King. From this we can see that the core of Christian faith is not about agreeing with a set of beliefs, but rather, gaining a right understanding of who Jesus is, that leads to a right relationship with Him.

EXPLORE MORE

Read John 5 v 24, Ephesians 2 v 1-5, Colossians 2 v 13-14. What does it mean to be "dead" according to these verses? What does it mean to be "alive"?

John 5 v 24: To be "dead" is to remain under God's condemnation because you have not listened to and believed in Jesus; to be "alive" is to receive eternal life because you hear the word of Jesus and believe the one who sent Jesus.

Ephesians 2 v 1-5: To be "dead" is to be living in your transgressions and sins, following the ways of this world, gratifying the cravings of your sinful nature and under God's wrath (v 1-3); to be "alive" is to receive God's mercy in Jesus Christ and be saved (v 4-5).

Colossians 2 v 13-14: To be "dead" is to be in your sins; to be "alive" is to be forgiven of your sins in Christ.

In the following verses, what do we discover about the way the physical death of a Christian is different from that of a non-Christian?

1 Corinthians 15 v 20: The death of a Christian is described as "falling asleep"—this is because physical death will be followed by resurrection, just as Christ Himself rose from the dead, and just as He raised the daughter of the synagogue ruler back to life in Matthew 9.

1 Corinthians 15 v 55-57: Death for Christians has lost its sting (it is harmless), because through Jesus Christ, God has given Christians victory over sin and the power of the law to condemn us.

Philippians 1 v 21-23: Paul described the prospect of his own death as "gain" (v 21) because he would then be with Christ (v 23). All these New Testament passages show us that the experience of death is transformed into something utterly different—harmless, hopeful, and something we need not fear—when a person becomes a Christian.

Why is the experience of death transformed for a Christian (see Hebrews 2 v 9)? When Jesus died on the cross, He tasted death for everyone. This was God's grace to us; Jesus experienced true death—God's condemnation of sin—so that we would not have to.

Now explain Jesus' words in v 25-26. "Whoever believes in me will live, even though they die" (v 25b). Jesus is saying that when Christians die, they will immediately enter into all the joys of eternal life—this is what Paul describes as "gain" in Philippians 1 v 21.

"Whoever lives by believing in me will never die" (v 26). Jesus is saying that because Christians have been forgiven through His death on the cross, when their bodies die what they experience will be like falling asleep, rather than true death. This is because Christians have been forgiven of their sins and are no longer under God's condemnation—what Paul describes as the "sting" of death. So it is true that Christians die (v 25b—their bodies die), but they never die (v 26—they are never condemned by God).

8. Jesus knew that "this illness [would] not end in death" (v 4, see also v 11-13). Why, then, did Jesus weep, do you think (v 33-35)? Jesus had no reason to mourn Lazarus' death because He knew that He would raise him from the dead (v 11-14). But Jesus wept because Mary and the Jews were weeping (v 33). Their heartbreak caused Him pain. It always hurts God to see us suffer—even though it is always part of His plan. The painful consequences of sin and death in the world grieve God. And sin and death should grieve us too. People without any hope in the face of death sometimes try to make it something natural, normal and even beautiful, but the Bible always presents death as an enemy of humankind, although of course it is a defeated enemy.

9. What did the Jews conclude about Jesus?

- **verse 36:** They thought Jesus was weeping because He had lost someone He loved—they clearly did not think Jesus would raise His beloved friend from the dead. In other words, they did not doubt that He loved Lazarus, but they did doubt His power.

- **verse 37:** Some of the Jews reacted differently. They were sceptical of Jesus' tears. They doubted His love for Lazarus because they thought that He could have prevented his death: "Could not he who opened the eyes of the blind man have kept this man from dying?" They did not doubt His power, but they did doubt His love.

10. APPLY: What can we learn from Martha and Mary about how to respond to death and bereavement?

Like Martha and Mary, we all handle grief differently, and that's okay. What is important is that we cling to Jesus and that we trust Him. Martha and Mary knew that Jesus loved Lazarus and that He could have prevented his death. They didn't question His love or His power. They just trusted Him. These women have set a beautiful example for us to follow.

11. APPLY: What can we learn from the Jews about how not to respond to tragedy?

Like the Jews, we may doubt either God's power or His goodness, instead of just trusting that He is both good and powerful. However, God gives us glimpses of His purposes in allowing suffering, if we are willing to look for them. We should realise that when He has allowed suffering in the past, it has always been for a good reason. So, for example, Jesus allowed Lazarus to die so that His disciples and others (John 12 v 11) would believe in Him and have eternal life. One man died so that many would live! But, when their brother was lying motionless in the tomb, Martha and Mary couldn't have known about Jesus' plan. We need to trust God, even when we don't have the answers to our questions.

12. APPLY: How are Jesus' words to Martha in verses 23-26 both a comfort and a warning to those who have suffered loss?

Comfort: There is hope! Hope of eternal life after death for those who believe in Jesus. What a consolation that is to us when a Christian dies. *Warning:* But it is also a solemn warning to put our trust in Jesus. Death is real and imminent— we are reminded of this when a loved one dies. And without Jesus, there is no hope of life beyond the grave.

Note: Be aware that some people in the group may be struggling with the issue of what has happened to a friend or relative who has died without trusting in Jesus Christ for the forgiveness of their sins. In responding to this, we must be careful not to compromise the clear teaching of the Bible about what happens to unbelievers. Nor should we offer false hope or vague possibilities about the fate of those who have died. It is far better to help someone struggling with this issue to trust in the perfect goodness of God. Mention Abraham's great statement of faith in God's character—"Will not the Judge of all the earth do right?" (Genesis 18 v 25). Reassure them that at the last day everything will be understood fully and accurately. Revelation 21 v 4 tells us that in eternity there will be no more grief or pain—it seems that Christians will be at peace about things which deeply upset us now.

13. What did Jesus mean when He said that Martha would "see the glory of God" (v 40)? How is God glorified through this miracle? The precise words that Jesus quotes in v 40 are not mentioned previously. However, Jesus is probably referring to His conversation with Martha in v 21-27, when He claimed to be able to give life to those who believe. When Jesus raised Lazarus from the dead, God's life-giving power—His glory—was seen. God is glorified by His Son's power over death.

14. APPLY: Where can we see God's glory most fully displayed? See also 12 v 23-24, 31-33. 12 v 23-24: Jesus would be glorified in His death on the cross. His one death would produce life in the many who would come to believe in Him. John 12 v 31-33: Jesus' death drove Satan out and drew all men to Himself. Jesus' power over death is most clearly seen in His own resurrection. Jesus is life (v 25) and death could not master Him. That is glorious!

• **What difference should that make to our lives this week?** There are many directions which the discussion could take: Are we passing on this message, which is the only hope for humans in the face of death? Do we grieve differently for Christian brothers and sisters? How do we cope with the prospect of ageing and our

own approaching death? What is the big thing that we live for? If we have children, what are our greatest hopes and ambitions for them? Etc.

OPTIONAL EXTRA
Research beliefs about what happens after death, and share these with your group. You could find out what other religions teach, and what kind of beliefs existed in the ancient world before the resurrection of Christ. Why not ask someone in the group to do this eg: if they have someone in their family who is, say, a Buddhist? Or find some quotations on the subject of death. Bring these to the group and compare them with the Christian hope of a bodily resurrection and eternal life in a renewed universe.

8 John 20 v 1-18
FAITH THAT SHARES THE GOOD NEWS

THE BIG IDEA

Jesus was raised from the dead—the evidence urges us to believe that; we should not only rejoice in the hope that this historic event has brought into our lives, but also share the fantastic news with others in obedience to Jesus, as Mary did.

SUMMARY

The stone had been rolled away, revealing an empty tomb. It was empty of everything but the strips of linen and the burial cloth that had been around Jesus' head and body. This is evidence that Jesus' body had not been stolen, but raised. What thief would waste precious time unwrapping the body and then leaving the linen, the most valuable item in the tomb, neatly folded up? Although this was enough to convince John, it was not enough to persuade Mary. But Mary's unbelief dissolved with her tears when she saw Jesus and recognised His voice. Jesus discouraged her from clinging to Him because He wanted to prepare her for the fact that He was going. She would no longer see Him or hear Him in a physical sense. Rather, she would continue His work by proclaiming the good news after He returned to heaven.

Note: There is a lot of confusion about the nature of Jesus' relationship with Mary Magdalene. Most of this confusion has been caused by Dan Brown's book, *The Da Vinci Code*, in which he suggests that Jesus married and had children by her. But there is no biblical basis for this suggestion. On the contrary, in the Bible the only time

Jesus is recorded speaking to Mary is in this passage—and it is to discourage her from holding onto Him! Other than that, all we know of their relationship is that Jesus had driven seven demons from her and that she had supported Him in His ministry along with several other women (Luke 8 v 1-3); also, that she had been present when He died (John 19 v 25).

GUIDANCE ON QUESTIONS

1. When something extraordinary happens to you, do you tend to talk about it or keep it to yourself? The purpose of this question is primarily to encourage discussion and to prepare people for the main message of the study—that the resurrection is an extraordinary truth that we cannot keep to ourselves!

2. Looking at verses 1-9, what evidence is there in this passage that Jesus was physically raised from the dead?

- **v 1 (compare Mark 16 v 1-4; Matthew 28 v 2):** He writes that "the stone had been removed from the entrance" of the tomb. This stone was "very large" (Mark 16 v 4) and was designed to seal the tomb permanently. No wonder getting inside was such a problem for the group of women who went to anoint Jesus' body (Mark 16 v 3). And so in Matthew 28 v 2, we read that an angel intervened—and caused a violent earthquake!

- **v 2:** Mary's words, "they have taken the Lord out of the tomb", suggest the tomb was empty—there was no dead body!

• **v 3–7:** The tomb was empty, except for the strips of linen and the burial cloth that had been around Jesus' head. This is significant because what thief would waste precious time unwrapping the body and then leaving the linen, the most valuable item in the tomb, neatly folded up? Notice the detail in these verses: "Both were running" (v 4); "he bent over" (v 5); "the cloth was still lying in its place, separate from the linen" (v 7). These events were clearly reported by an eyewitness—John, the writer of this account, was the "other disciple". (**Note:** John often refers to himself in the third person, as in John 21 v 24.)

3. Compare the ways in which "the other disciple" and Mary reacted to the empty tomb.

• **The other disciple:** He believed that Jesus had been raised from the dead on the basis of these three pieces of evidence alone. He had not yet understood the words of Jesus or the prophecies in the Old Testament Scriptures which spoke of the resurrection (v 9). But what he saw was enough to convince him. He didn't understand why Jesus' death and resurrection had been God's plan all along—or even that it had been planned. But he believed that it had happened.

• **Mary:** John does not tell us that Mary saw all that he saw on her first visit to the tomb. However, according to Luke 24 v 3 and Mark 16 v 5, she went inside. But rather than believing, she assumed that Jesus had been taken away (v 2, 13 and 15). Mary's assumption is understandable. But it was an assumption that ignored the evidence in this passage. If Jesus' dead and decaying body had been stolen, whether by the political or religious authorities, why would they have removed the strips of linen and the burial cloth? And why would grave robbers have left the most valuable item—the expensive linen—behind? Only the resurrection explains why these things were found in the tomb. But it was not enough to convince Mary. Even the presence of the angels could not convince her (v 12-13; see also Mark 16 v 4-8). Like Thomas in John 20 v 24-29, nothing but a personal encounter with Jesus would convince her that He had risen (v 16).

4. APPLY: At first, Mary failed to believe in the resurrection despite the evidence she had seen. Why is it still important to have evidence for the resurrection?

God has given us clear evidence for the resurrection, so that no one can say that Christian faith is blind, or Christian belief unreasonable. It is important that Christians know that their faith is founded on historical facts which are objectively true. Otherwise, all we are left with is what we feel like believing, and that can change! It is important because it reflects the character of God, who is trustworthy and true. It is important because the Christian faith is not about beliefs that you like, but beliefs that are true. This is why John wrote his account of Jesus' life (John 20 v 31).

• **Why isn't the evidence sufficient for people to believe, do you think?** Mary could not (or would not) believe, despite being given proof. Like her, many people simply will not believe, no matter what we say to convince them. This shouldn't surprise us—the New Testament says faith itself is a gift from God (Ephesians 2 v 8). The New Testament also teaches that we cannot accept God's message without the Holy Spirit (see 1 Corinthians 2 v 12-14). It is impossible for people to believe without the help of the Holy Spirit.

5. APPLY: People who don't believe in the resurrection need other theories to explain the disappearance of Jesus' body from the tomb. What explanations are commonly given? How can you use the evidence in this passage to contradict these theories?

- *Jesus' body was stolen, either by the political or religious authorities, the disciples or grave robbers:* As we have seen, it is unlikely that anyone other than a grave robber would have unwrapped a decomposing corpse. And grave robbers would not have left the costly linen behind! If the authorities had stolen the body, why did they not produce it and so stop the spread of Christianity? If the disciples had stolen the body, why were they willing to suffer and die for a lie?

- *Jesus didn't really die:* According to the eye-witnesses, He was crucified. The soldiers did not break his legs to speed up His death because they knew He was already dead. Instead, to make sure, they pierced His side with a spear. His body was then wrapped with strips of linen and buried in a tomb. But then, three days later, without any medical help, it is suggested that Jesus recovered enough to remove the very large stone and walk free! This idea was too absurd for anyone to suggest at the time. Even resurrection from the dead is more believable than this ridiculous theory!

- *The story was simply made up:* If you hold to this theory, you still need to explain the following: Why were the disciples willing to die for a made-up story? How do you explain the four Gospel accounts, each different in the details but each agreeing with the others? What happened to Jesus? Why was the story of the resurrection never refuted at the time?

EXPLORE MORE
Read 1 Corinthians 15 v 12-28. What is the significance of the resurrection? Or, to put it another way, what would it mean if Jesus had never been raised from the dead? Base your answers on:

- **v 14-16:** If Jesus had never been raised from the dead, then the apostles' were false witnesses (v 15). And if their testimony (that they had seen the resurrected Jesus) was false, then their message had no power—it was useless (v 14).

- **v 17-19:** Not only that, but our faith in that message is useless too! Death is the final punishment for sin. So if Jesus didn't rise from the dead, we can safely conclude that He was a sinner. In that case, He didn't have any authority to forgive sin or to give life—"you are still in your sins" (v 17).

- **v 22-26:** Jesus' resurrection proves that He reigns. He rules over every other authority and power—even death.

6. Read Luke 8 v 2-3. What can we learn about Mary Magdalene here?
She had been demon-possessed. But after Jesus had cured her of the evil spirits she became an active participant in His ministry. She may well have been a wealthy woman since she was able to give Jesus and His disciples financial support. Her companion, Joanna, certainly was—her husband was the "manager of Herod's household"! But the important thing to notice is that Mary had personally experienced Jesus' deliverance and, as a result, had devoted her time and her money to His ministry.

7. How is Mary's deep love for Jesus seen in this story (v 10-18)? Try to imagine how Mary was feeling at this point.

Three days earlier the man who had rescued her, and to whom she had devoted her life, had been crucified. She had watched Him die (John 19 v 25). And now she could not even tend to His body—she could not visit the tomb in which His body lay. Her tears show us the depth of her grief and love. "Mary stood outside the tomb crying" (v 11)—it is a heart-breaking and beautiful picture. But her love for Jesus is also seen in her determination to fetch His body: "Tell me where you have put him, and I will get him" (v 15). This would have been a dangerous thing to do, and yet she doesn't even seem to consider that. Her love for Jesus was greater than her fear.

8. At what point does Mary believe that Jesus is alive (v 14-16)? Read verses 24-28. How does Thomas' experience compare with Mary's? Even though Mary's tears are moving, they are also unnecessary. The angels and Jesus both highlight this: "Woman, why are you crying?" (v 13, 15) She has no reason to cry—Jesus is alive! But despite the evidence, Mary is not sure what has happened to Jesus' body: "I don't know where they have put him" (v 13). Even when she sees Jesus, she doesn't recognise Him, perhaps because her tears have blurred her sight, or perhaps because in His resurrection state He is not entirely or immediately recognisable. It is only when she hears Him say her name that she believes He is alive. Like Mary, Thomas only believes once he has seen Jesus. So Jesus says to him: "Because you have seen me, you have believed; blessed are those who have not seen and yet have believed" (John 20 v 29). We can't see the resurrected Jesus. But we do have the evidence. And we will be "blessed" if we believe!

9. Jesus' words "Do not hold on to me" (v 17a) seem a bit heartless. Why do you think Jesus says this to Mary? Jesus explained why Mary was not to cling to Him: "for I have not yet ascended to the Father". Jesus wasn't going to go yet—she didn't need to cling to Him as though He was. But He was going to go eventually. And so Jesus said this to teach Mary to relate to Him in a spiritual rather than a physical way, and to prepare her to live by faith and not by sight.

10. What does He command her to do instead? "Go instead to my brothers and tell them, 'I am ascending to my Father and your Father, to my God and your God'" (v 17). Here, Jesus is speaking of His future ascension to heaven, recorded in Acts 1 v 9-11, which would happen about 40 days later. Instead of clinging to Jesus, Mary was to tell others that He had risen and was going to return to His Father's throne to reign. Instead of travelling with and supporting Jesus as He proclaimed the good news, she was to proclaim it herself!

11. Look at verse 19 and Luke 24 v 11. What things must have made it hard for Mary to do as Jesus said? Imagine how dangerous it would have been to proclaim that Jesus had risen! Jesus had been hated, persecuted and crucified. What would they do to His followers? Matthew 27 v 62-66 makes it clear that the Jewish and Roman authorities were determined to prevent any story of a resurrection from getting out. The disciples were fully aware of the dangers— they locked themselves inside "for fear of the Jews" (John 20 v 19). And imagine how absurd it would have sounded. Would anyone believe Mary? According to Luke 24 v 11, not even the disciples believed it because her "words seemed to them like nonsense"! But Mary did obey Jesus (v 18).

12. APPLY: In what way does this story show how we should relate to the risen Lord in this world? We all long for the time when we will be with the Lord—when we will see His face and hear His voice, as Mary did. As a young Christian I wondered why I couldn't go to heaven immediately. But then I realised that God had left me on earth for one reason—to tell others about Jesus' life, death and resurrection. We cannot enjoy being in the physical presence of Jesus yet, but we can—and must— proclaim the good news so that others can come to know Him as their risen Lord and Saviour too.

13. APPLY: Why do we so often fail to tell others about Jesus' death and resurrection? There are many reasons why we fail to spread the good news. Often, we doubt that anyone will believe it—we think that it will seem like nonsense to them. What little confidence we have in this powerful message! Or we may be afraid that we will be persecuted. Currently in the western world, we do not face the same dangers that Mary faced. Mary could have been risking her life—we only stand to lose our reputations or our relationships. But aren't those worth risking for the Lord?

⊻

- **Which groups in our society can Christians be fearful of? How can we reach these people?**

- **How can we bring the subject of the resurrection into our everyday conversations with non-Christians?** Often we make too much of talking about Christ, become nervous and don't do it! Encourage your group to think of talking about Jesus as being as natural to a

Christian as talking about a film or fashion or holidays. Give them time to think about ways in which resurrection and eternal life can be worked into everyday conversations.

OPTIONAL REVIEW SESSION
You may like to spend an additional study reviewing the contents of this Good Book Guide with your group. Use the following questions and comments to encourage and help discussion:

- **Who were the women of faith in the New Testament? What strikes you about them?** In many ways, these were not impressive women. They were a group of outcasts, including pagans and sinners. Even the prominent Mary Magdalene had been demon-possessed and Mary the mother of Jesus called herself "humble". And yet these women impressed Jesus most because they trusted Him.

- **What can we learn from each of these beautiful characters?** Get people in your group to recall the main teaching points of each session.

- **Many of these women suffered greatly. What do they teach us about how to respond to suffering?** Many of these women endured much testing and suffering. It was through their affliction— through having to trust, to pray and to persevere—that they grew to become such beautiful characters. In fact, suffering plays an important part in the maturing of faith. God uses it, not to punish us, but to grow us.

- **Each session has focused on one aspect of faith. What should our relationship with Jesus look like as a whole?** We cannot have a relationship with Jesus unless we know Him. Mary, His mother, knew God—His character, His ways, His promises, and His plans.

Ultimately, we need to know Jesus as our risen Lord and Saviour. Knowing Him means loving Him for His forgiveness, trusting Him when we suffer, and persevering in prayer when He tests us. It involves serving Him and telling others about Him but, more importantly, it involves listening to Him—living by His every word!

Get group members to share what they have learned and how they have been helped and challenged by the sessions. Perhaps ask two or three people to prepare a short "testimony" about how they have grown over the past eight weeks. Here are a few more discussion questions:

- **Which of these women do you identify with most? Why?**
- **Which character do you want to be more like? Why?**
- **What practical steps can you take to develop faith like this?**

Also available in the Good Book Guide series...

OLD TESTAMENT

Ruth: Poverty and plenty
4 studies. ISBN: 9781905564910

Ezekiel: The God of glory
6 studies. ISBN: 9781904889274

Jonah: The depths of grace
6 studies. ISBN: 9781907377433

NEW TESTAMENT

Mark 1-8: The coming King
10 studies. ISBN: 9781904889281

1 Thessalonians: Living to please God 7 studies. ISBN: 9781904889533

1 Peter: Living in the real world
5 studies. ISBN: 9781904889496

2 Timothy: Faithful to the end
7 studies. ISBN: 9781905564569

TOPICAL

Soul songs: Psalms
6 studies. ISBN: 9781904889960

Biblical womanhood 10 studies.
ISBN: 9781904889076

Biblical manhood 10 studies.
ISBN: 9781904889977

Experiencing God 6 studies.
ISBN: 9781906334437

Women of faith from the OT
8 studies. ISBN: 9781904889526

The Holy Spirit 8 studies.
ISBN: 9781905564217

Contentment 6 studies.
ISBN: 9781905564668

The Apostles' Creed 10 studies.
ISBN: 9781905564415

thegoodbook
COMPANY
Opening up the Bible

At The Good Book Company, we are dedicated to helping Christians and local churches grow. We believe that God's growth process always starts with hearing clearly what He has said to us through His timeless word—the Bible.

Ever since we opened our doors in 1991, we have been striving to produce resources that honour God in the way the Bible is used. We have grown to become an international provider of user-friendly resources to the Christian community, with believers of all backgrounds and denominations using our Bible studies, books, evangelistic resources, DVD-based courses and training events.

We want to equip ordinary Christians to live for Christ day by day, and churches to grow in their knowledge of God, their love for one another, and the effectiveness of their outreach.

Call us for a discussion of your needs or visit one of our local websites for more information on the resources and services we provide.

UK & Europe: www.thegoodbook.co.uk
Australia: www.thegoodbook.com.au
New Zealand: www.thegoodbook.co.nz
North America: www.thegoodbook.com

UK & Europe: 0333 123 0880
Australia: (02) 6100 4211
New Zealand (+64) 3 343 1990
North America: 866 244 2165

www.christianityexplored.org

Our partner site is a great place for those exploring the Christian faith, with a clear explanation of the good news, powerful testimonies and answers to difficult questions.

One life. What's it all about?